Lynn Triplett

AN INTRODUCTION
TO JAPAN

AN INTRODUCTION

TO JAPAN

by Herschel Webb

COLUMBIA UNIVERSITY PRESS
NEW YORK AND LONDON

This book has been sponsored by the Japan Society, a private, nonprofit, nonpolitical association of Americans and Japanese who desire to help bring the peoples of the United States and Japan closer together in their appreciation and understanding of each other and each other's way of life. Offices of the Society are located at 18 East 50th Street, New York City.

PREFACE

An Introduction to Japan has been prepared and published under the auspices of the Japan Society in an effort to meet a growing interest in Japan and Japanese-American relationships on the part of American colleges, schools, and adult education groups. In a sense the present volume is the successor to the *Japan Society Syllabus,* last published in 1937. Rather than prepare a new edition of the *Syllabus,* however, the editors have felt it desirable to begin afresh and to issue a completely new volume, which would not only reflect the great changes that have taken place in Japan in the intervening years but also take into account the fundamental alteration in the relationship between Japan and the United States from one of rivalry between two mutually distrustful powers to the far more complex interdependent relationship of today.

Readings and films listed at the end of each section are merely suggestions and are not intended to comprise an exhaustive bibliography. *Japan,* edited by Hugh Borton (Ithaca, Cornell University Press, 1951), is a convenient and reliable source of information on all phases of Japanese life and affairs. For further materials the reader is referred to the best short bibliography on Japan, *A Selected List of Books and Articles on Japan in English, French, and German,* revised and enlarged edition, compiled by Hugh Borton, Serge Elisséeff,

William W. Lockwood, and John C. Pelzel (Harvard University Press, 1954).

The chapter entitled "Economic Life" is based on a study written for the Japan Society by Mr. Harlan E. Youel.

The author wishes to acknowledge the courteous assistance given him by Miss Miwa Kai and Mr. Philip Yampolsky of the East Asiatic Library, Columbia University, and Mrs. Mildred Ostler of the Lincoln (Nebraska) City Library. Among others who read the manuscript, particular thanks are due to Nadine Murayama and Katharine Wells for the many excellent suggestions they made while this work was in progress.

The chapter decorations are the work of Charles M. Saito. The map of Japan was prepared by Vaughn S. Gray.

H. W.

February, 1957

CONTENTS

CONTENTS

AN INTRODUCTION
TO JAPAN

NOTE ON PRONUNCIATION OF JAPANESE AND JAPANESE ORTHOGRAPHY

Consonants in Japanese have generally the same sound as in English, except that *g* is always hard. Vowels are as in Italian or as in the musical scale: *a* as in *fa, i* as in *mi, e* as in *re, o* as in *do; u* is like *oo* in *boot*. There is an almost even stress on every syllable, a syllable consisting of a consonant-vowel combination. A few syllables end with *n,* for example, the first syllable of *Man'yô-shû.* Vowels marked with a circumflex (Kantô, Kyôto) have approximately twice the time value of unmarked vowels.

Because of generally established usage, certain proper nouns are not marked. For readers who may be interested in knowing the pronunciation, however, these are the names of the islands —Hokkaidô, Honshû, Kyûshû, and Ryûkyû—and of the cities —Tôkyô, Ôsaka, Kôbe, and Kyôto. The *y* in these words is in effect a consonant: the *kyô* of Tôkyô is one syllable, and Kyûshû is pronounced Cue-shoo. Double consonants are both pronounced. In vowel combinations such as *ai* both are pronounced, but rapidly, so that the sound is similar to the pronoun *I* in English.

All Japanese and Chinese personal names are written according to the Oriental practice—family name first.

JAPAN AND THE
UNITED STATES

THE PAST DECADE

Never before in history has the relationship between the United States and Japan been so close as during the past ten years. Following the Second World War Japan, in theory at least, was occupied and controlled by thirteen Allied Powers, which sought to demilitarize her and to encourage democratic tendencies among her people. However, since the thirteen Powers by agreement acted only through the American government and a Supreme Commander in Tokyo (also an American), Japan's postwar treatment was largely in American hands. Thus it came about that the United States assumed primary responsibility for the disarming of Japan, the initiation of political, economic, and social reforms, the carrying out of relief measures, and even the defense of the country.

With the coming into force of the peace treaty in 1952 the occupation formally ended, and Japan regained her full sovereignty. At the same time, however, responsible leaders in both countries were well aware that without any armed forces of her own and without outside help Japan might become a power vacuum, open to communist subversion from within and Soviet and Red Chinese aggression from without. Accordingly, the two countries negotiated simultaneously with the peace treaty a security treaty under which the United States is to keep armed forces in and about Japan until the latter can provide adequately for her own defense.

These two treaties, together with an administrative agreement spelling out in detail the status of the American forces in Japan (1952), a Mutual Defense Assistance Pact (1954), and a Treaty of Friendship, Commerce, and Navigation (1953), form the present basis of Japan's relations with the United States.

Treaties and pacts alone, however, do not wholly explain the importance of each country to the other. To America Japan is a bastion of strength against communist Asia, and the northern anchor of America's westernmost line of defense, which runs from Hokkaido to Australia. Further, with her highly developed society, modern industrial complex, and technological skills Japan stands in a special position to lend stability to the rest of Asia. To Japan the relationship has more than a military significance: the United States is a major source for her imports, a major market for her exports, a provider of dollar aid, and a powerful political ally that can help her to achieve status in the world.

SOME PROBLEMS

Public pronouncements from both sides of the Pacific attest to the willingness of both Japan and the United States to stand together politically, militarily, and economically. In the United States, however, these pronouncements have all too often bred either an overconfident belief that the current amity will continue automatically or an apathetic attitude that whatever happens to Japan is of no great concern to Americans. If only to counteract these prevailing moods, a note of caution is in order. Despite the cooperation of the two governments and evidences of friendliness between the two peoples, some friction does exist. Some of the more noteworthy causes are indicated below.

1. The rearmament of Japan is regarded in the United States as a necessary and sensible means of reducing the communist threat. Most Japanese, weary of war and apprehensive that Japan may again become a battlefield, see the rearmament issue in an entirely different light. Many fear a resurgence of Japanese militarism. Still more wishfully think that disarmed neutrality offers them a better chance of survival in another war than active belligerence on either side.

2. A particular irritant to the Japanese has been the American practice of conducting nuclear weapon tests in the central Pacific. Whereas the Japanese government has accepted the need for these tests realistically, it has done so only in the face of bitter and vociferous opposition from the public at large. This opposition is based in large part on fear of fall-outs and contamination of Japan's vital fishing catch as well as the tragic memory of Hiroshima and Nagasaki.

3. Despite a generally good record of behavior by American troops in Japan, their continued presence eleven years after the surrender unavoidably causes resentment among Japanese. Specific grievances have been the extraterritorial privileges granted to the American security forces, prostitution near military installations, and a small but well-publicized number of occupation babies of mixed race. There is also a fear that the national way of life is becoming overly Americanized.

4. The territories which Japan lost as a result of military defeat included the Ryukyu and Bonin Islands, which the Japanese claim were not acquired by military aggression. Irredentist antagonism toward the United States, the present administering authority, is a natural consequence. However, the strategic importance of Okinawa in the Ryukyu group makes it unlikely that the United States will be willing fully to satisfy Japanese territorial desires, at least in the foreseeable future.

5. Possibly the most immediate danger of friction between America and Japan lies in the conflicting views of the two countries on Japanese trade with Communist China. The disagreement is a clear-cut instance of the possible incompatibilities between Japanese economic demands on the one hand and American military policy on the other. In the long run, it seems likely that Japan will need mainland goods and markets which are now prohibited under American pressure. Since Chinese demands for Japanese products are to a large extent limited to goods that could be used to build up communist military strength, it is extremely unlikely that the United States, under the present circumstances of international politics, will take kindly to renewal of full trade between the two countries. Positions so flatly contradictory as these might eventually lead to a serious strain in Japanese-American relations.

6. While at the present time trade rivalry between Japan and the United States is not strong, certain Japanese exports to the United States, notably cotton textiles, tuna, and pottery, have caused concern among American producers and led to pressure on Congress for increased tariffs or the establishment of import quotas. Dependent as they are on international trade, the Japanese are extremely sensitive to all such moves which

directly affect their livelihood. It appears likely that trade problems will be an irritant in relations between the two countries for some years to come.

It should not be overlooked that there exist on both sides of the Pacific certain groups that either deliberately seek or unwittingly abet friction between the United States and Japan. Chief of these on the Japanese side are 1) a small but fanatical communist minority, which can be expected to exaggerate and exploit every difference of opinion between Japan and the United States; 2) the socialist opposition, which because of the pro-American policies of the present government is frequently forced into the tactical position of making proposals which have an anti-American cast; and 3) a considerable number of the intelligentsia, who are inclined to regard American cultural achievements as inferior to those of Europe and Asia.

On the other side, despite the fact that organized anti-Japanese sentiment in the United States disappeared after the Second World War, there still exist in this country certain groups that could bring about a deterioration in the relations between the two nations. Lobbyists for certain Southern textile manufacturers, for example, have achieved state legislation designed to encourage crippling boycotts of competing goods from Japan. There exist, in addition, high-tariff interests, the success of whose efforts might well wreck Japan's already precarious economy, and isolationist groups, whose desire to withdraw from Far Eastern commitments raises Japanese fears that Japan will be abandoned and left to face the Soviet Union and Red China alone.

Nevertheless, it must be granted that most Americans and Japanese appear to be satisfied with the present close alignment of the two countries. If some Americans have doubts about the ability of the Japanese to maintain their new-found political liberties and to avoid a resurgence of militaristic expansionism, they are at least content to adopt a wait-and-see attitude. If certain Japanese groups would prefer to adopt a course of neutralism rather than alignment with the United States, the majority of voters up to the present have been willing to support a government strongly committed to the West. So long as the Japanese people remain convinced that their present international position offers them the best hope of avoiding war and hunger, two omnipresent fears that far overshadow the fear of communism, Japan can be expected to continue close cooperation with the United States. Should they become disillusioned in this regard, their fear of war may breed further neutralism toward the East-West struggle, and their fear of hunger might easily lead them to attempt a solution in totalitarianism, be it of the right or of the left.

READINGS

Reischauer, Edwin O. *The United States and Japan*. Cambridge, Harvard University Press, 1950.

Reischauer, Edwin O., and others. *Japan and America Today*. Stanford, Stanford University Press, 1953.

LAND AND
PEOPLE

LOCATION, SIZE, AND REGIONS

Japan consists of four main islands and many adjacent smaller ones, a total land area of 142,300 square miles. (Montana, among American states, compares most closely, with 145,878 square miles.) Honshu is the central island and Hokkaido lies due north of it. Shikoku is south of western Honshu across the Inland Sea, and Kyushu completes the group at the southwest extremity. The archipelago spans a range of latitude from roughly 30° to 46° north (approximately New Orleans to Minneapolis or Jacksonville to Montreal). Honshu, with five eighths of the total area and three quarters of the population, is divided for convenience into at least three unofficial regions —northern, central, and western—each of which has its own distinguishing geographical, climatic, and economic characteristics. Northern Honshu extends roughly northward from about the Tokyo Bay area and is commonly referred to as the Tôhoku, or northeast region. Central Honshu extends from the metropolitan areas of Tokyo and Yokohama to those of Osaka and Kobe. The Tokyo Bay cities dominate an area of central Honshu known as the Kantô, which is the governmental and commercial center of the nation. Kyoto, the old capital, and the neighboring industrial and shipping centers of Osaka and Kobe are situated in the other major region of central Honshu, the Kansai. Another great metropolitan area, that of Nagoya, lies about midway between Kantô and Kansai. Western Honshu is a narrow peninsula thrust westward from the Kansai district between the Inland Sea and the Japan Sea and is called Chûgoku.

The islands of Japan arch around two sides of the Japan Sea, which separates them from Korea and the Maritime Province of the Soviet Union. Japan, like England, prizes her "splendid isolation" from her continental neighbors, though the isolation in Japan's case is more complete. One cannot, after all, swim the Korea Strait—120 miles—which separates western Honshu from Korea. Russia's Far Eastern port of Vladivostok is over four hundred miles across the Japan Sea from northern Japan. In the extreme northeast, postwar occupation by the Soviet Union of islands in the Kurile chain, almost within earshot of eastern Hokkaido, brings a traditional enemy closer to Japanese home ground than ever before in Japan's modern history.

Limited by her seashores and by international agreements, Japan's capacity for feeding her people is further restricted by the ruggedness of the terrain. About three fourths of the country is nonarable, that is, too steeply graded for crop cultivation. The population, increasing steadily over the past hundred years, long ago outstripped the available agricultural land and made it impossible for Japan to be even quantitatively self-sufficient in basic necessities. Industry and overseas commerce will always be required to redress the balance. It is sheer necessity that has made Japan a maritime nation.

Note: Okinawa and the Ryukyu Islands
below the 27th parallel are administered by
the United States under treaty. Certain of
the southern Kurile Islands are in dispute
with the U.S.S.R.

Japan is an Asian nation by tradition; her cultural roots must be sought in Korea, China, and India. Her economic life still continues to be conditioned by the circumstances of Far Eastern commerce. Yet it is of major importance to Japan's recent history that she has become to an increasing degree a Pacific nation, linked by transoceanic commerce to the community of nations that includes Australia, New Zealand, Chile, Mexico, the United States, and Canada.

CLIMATE

Japan's latitude makes for a temperate climate. Temperatures tend to range higher than in similar latitudes in eastern North America due to the influence of the Japan Current, a tropical stream that flows northeast along Japan's east (Pacific) coast. The same current accounts for the higher average winter temperatures south and east of Japan's central mountain ranges than along the Japan Sea coast.

Rainfall is heavy, ranging from 40 to 100 inches annually. The Pacific coast has strikingly heavier precipitation than the Japan Sea area. Snowfall is frequent and heavy in the latter area and in northern Japan. Seasonal variations are more or less well marked in all parts of the country, particularly in the central and northern portions. All seasons are humid and both summers and winters are, as a consequence, unpleasant. Rainfall is heaviest during a dispiriting season of June and July known as the *tsuyu*. Autumn, with bright, crisp weather, is delightful. Winters, except in the far north, rarely approach the miseries associated with that time of year in mid-continental or eastern America. Spring is pleasant, though damp, and is spectacular more for its bursts of blossoms—plum, cherry, or peach—than for any sudden change from cold to warm weather.

TOPOGRAPHY

Japan's many mountain ranges have a fundamental economic significance. Useful in that they provide timber and make potentially cheap water power available, they are all but useless for habitation or farming. The Japanese islands are of volcanic origin and more than fifty active volcanoes remain, clustered most profusely in Hokkaido, central Honshu, and Kyushu. The highest altitudes, respectively, of these three areas are: Asahi-dake (or Taisetsu-zan), 7,513 feet above sea level; Fuji-san (Mt. Fuji), 12,395 feet; and Yae-shima, 6,348 feet.

Japan is the most actively volcanic region within the world's principal "earthquake belt," which rings the Pacific from New Zealand by way of Alaska to the Strait of Magellan. Seismographs record several thousand disturbances annually, though most of these are too weak to be destructive. Major earthquakes are not infrequent, however, and can be terrible destroyers of life and property. The Kantô earthquake of September 1, 1923, which took upwards of 40,000 lives, was one of the greatest natural disasters in man's recorded history.

There are few extensive plains in Japan, but these are of great economic importance; they support a substantial part of the population and provide much of the food supply. The largest of them is the Kantô plain adjoining Tokyo Bay; others of importance are the Kinki region, including the Kansai cities, and the Chikugo plain of northern Kyushu.

The complex coast line totals 17,150 miles (about twice that of the United States). Harbors are numerous; some of them,

including the two principal ones, Yokohama and Kobe, have
been dredged to permit access to ocean-going vessels.

POPULATION

The census of October, 1955, showed a total population for
Japan of 89,269,000 (43,856,000 were male and 45,414,000 female—a ratio of 96.6 males per 100 females).
The following table shows national totals and sex distribution for significant years.

Year	National Total	Males per 100 Females
1920	55,391,000	100.5
1930	63,872,000	101.1
1940	71,540,000	100.1
1945 (November)	72,455,000	89
1947	78,101,000	95.4
1950	83,200,000	96.2
1955 (October)	89,269,000	96.6

The proportion of urban population to the national total
rose from 18 percent in 1920 to 37.7 percent in 1940. Wartime
evacuation of cities and the destruction of urban housing resulted in a sharp drop in the figure to 28.7 percent in 1945;
but the postwar movement to cities has been equally remarkable (due in part to the resettlement of nationals repatriated
from Japan's former colonies and occupied territories), and
the ratio of urban population to the total now stands at 55.8
percent. Japan has six cities approaching or surpassing 1,000,000
in population and eighty-eight exceeding 100,000. Tokyo, the
capital, had 8,034,000 in 1955; Osaka had 2,547,000.

Japan's serious population problem may be comprehended

from three facts; the population has increased nearly threefold since the first modern census in 1872; despite a declining birth rate, lowered death rates have resulted in a constant rate of increase; finally, the present population density (226 per square kilometer in 1950, 247 in 1955), although less than in some areas of the world, permits little further expansion. There has in a sense been a population problem for centuries. Population pressure in the areas first settled accounted for the expansion of the Japanese people from their homelands in northern Kyushu, the Kansai, and Chûgoku districts, first to southern Kyushu and the Kantô and later to northern Honshu and the other islands of the group. Exploitation of marginal land in the centuries after all the main islands were settled afforded more room for population growth. Industrialization in the past century stimulated further growth by increasing the total national wealth, while overseas colonies before the war provided both a convenient source for commercial wealth and *lebensraum* for those Japanese who were enterprising enough to emigrate. Stripped of her colonies and with her industrial and commercial potential impaired by years of war, the nation is confronted with a sobering truth: the population is increasing steadily; the food supply is not.

READINGS

Cressey, George B. *Asia's Lands and Peoples; a Geography of One-Third the Earth and Two-Thirds Its People.* 2nd ed. New York, McGraw-Hill, 1951.

Japan Travel Bureau. *Japanese Tourist Library.* Tokyo. This collection of brochures on the culture of Japan is now in process of revision and expansion. For listing of books available and to be published, consult lists prepared by the Japan Travel Information Office, 10 Rockefeller Plaza, New York 20, N.Y.

Tourist Industry Division, Ministry of Transportation (ed.). *Japan, the Official Guide*. Revised. Tokyo, Japan Travel Bureau, 1952.

FILMS

Japan, Land and People. Coronet Films, Coronet Plaza, Chicago 1, Ill.

Japanese Fishing Village. Young America Films Inc., 18 E. 41st St., New York 17, New York.

Rice Farming in Japan, University of Michigan, Audio-Visual Education Center, 4028 Administration Building, Ann Arbor, Michigan.

So Small My Island. Pan American World Airways, 28–19 Bridge Plaza North, Long Island City, New York.

# HISTORY

In Japanese mythology, the nation's history began in 660 B.C., the year in which the first Emperor is said to have subdued the central provinces and ascended the throne. (The date was arrived at much later by calculating backwards in even Chinese calendrical cycles of sixty years; it means very little and in any case is considered at least six centuries too early for the origin of a real Japanese "dynasty.")

Archaeologists have found no traces in Japan of paleolithic settlement, but they agree in the identification of two neolithic cultures, the earlier of which seems to have existed from about the third millennium B.C. The second existed in the centuries just before the Christian era. Its artifacts seem to have belonged to a completely different race of people, though both cultures are conjectured to have come to Japan from northern Asia via Korea. Neither race should be called "Japanese." The Ainu stock of present-day northern Japan presumably descends from the earlier race, while the modern Japanese may be descended from a fusion of these two races and others perhaps from southern Asia or the islands of the southwest Pacific.

Archaeological evidence from early in the Christian era indicates a bronze age culture in contact with those of China and

Korea. This evidence is confirmed by Chinese texts from about
the same time in which Japan is spoken of as a collection of
"kingdoms," inhabited by a people intelligent, warlike, and
primitive. These developed a complex tribal society organized
around hereditary clans of officials, warriors, and artisans. One
such clan in one of the kingdoms came much later to be called
"Imperial" (the word and concept were Chinese). The earliest
Japanese accounts of their own history are legendary chronicles
of the origins of this clan (it was divine and descended from
heaven), and of its conquest of all the other Japanese kingdoms
and its organization of a centralized state.

Primitive Japanese religion conceived of the supernatural
as dwelling in all the objects and forces of nature. Supernatural
beings were called *kami* and the religion came to be called
Shintô, the "Way of the *kami.*" Statecraft in this age was an
aspect of religion, for it sought to control the *kami* behind the
forces of sun, rain, fire, and earthquake by means of ritual and
at the hands of a divine aristocracy and priesthood. The two
roles, governmental and priestly, were both hereditary in the
same families, so that Japan at the time was a theocracy.

THE SINICIZATION OF JAPAN: NARA (710–794)
AND HEIAN (794–1185) PERIODS

About 550 A.D., Buddhism entered Japan. After a century or
two, a major revolution—religious, social, cultural, and political
—made Japan a permanent part of the civilization of the
Chinese Far East, for Buddhism to the Japanese was the bearer
of all the attributes of Chinese civilization, then among the
world's most advanced. The Japanese studied Chinese archi-

tecture, sculpture, and painting, adapted the Chinese system of writing for the representation of their own language, founded schools on the continental pattern, and learned medicine, astronomy (and a fixed calendar), better methods for casting metals and fashioning tools, and Chinese music. The most complex component of Chinese culture was the organization of government and society, with the systems of land tenure, rents, and taxation that went with them. These the Japanese attempted valiantly to copy, and by 700 A.D. many of the forms of their political and economic life were Chinese imports. The ancient "divine" nobility did not pretend to shed their divinity, but they re-enforced their old religious authority with new concepts of loyalty and responsibility adopted from Confucian China. The emperor now had a double function: he was at once the chief priest and a secular ruler.

The Japanese failed to reproduce in their new state some of the most important institutions of the Chinese system. For one thing, the Chinese bureaucracy was in theory open to anyone, of whatever station, who could qualify in the competitive civil service examinations. The Japanese bureaucracy was in practice manned by aristocrats, descendants of the ancient priestly or military clans whose authority derived from sanctions of the native religion. In the Heian period (so called after the capital was moved from Nara to Heian-kyô, now Kyoto) divergence from purely Chinese culture grew noticeably. Buddhism, which remained the most important single religion, came more and more to be a faith for the people. Japanese artisans, having increased their skill at the crafts, developed them into something peculiarly Japanese (though it must be remembered that they never lost a fundamental Far Eastern character rooted in

China). A significant development was the shift of political power to a hereditary regency, or civil dictatorship, of the powerful Fujiwara family between the ninth and twelfth centuries. Though emperors continued to reign, their Fujiwara ministers effectively thwarted most of their urges to rule by taking advantage of the Throne's very divinity. A sacred ruler needed a mouthpiece to interpret his will to the people. If, as was frequently the case, the emperor was a minor related through his mother to the Fujiwara regent, the job of "interpreting" was naturally tantamount to sovereign authority.

Meanwhile, in the provinces, land that the seventh- and eighth-century law codes from China had placed in the hands of many small landholders tended to become concentrated in a few large estates. The means by which this was accomplished was similar to the European feudal practice of commendation of land to tax-exempt landlords by farmers more willing to pay local rent in exchange for protection than to pay taxes to an inept central government. These new, enlarged holdings were tax free owing to their owners' noble or ecclesiastical stations, and they came to constitute virtually autonomous states. The landholders came in time to form a new aristocracy, often called feudal from the dual political and economic nature of their tenure. They were a military aristocracy as well, fighting intermittently among themselves and engaging in constant warfare to expand the frontiers of Japanese settlement against the Ainus of the north. About 1150, two families of provincial nobility contended for supremacy. A general of the Taira clan first usurped civil authority previously reserved for Fujiwara ministers. Then after a civil war with the rival Minamoto clan —the heroic age of later poets and chroniclers—Taira supremacy collapsed, a Minamoto general named Yoritomo took command, and a new age of centralized military dictatorship had commenced.

MILITARY DICTATORSHIP TO 1600: KAMAKURA (1185–1333), MUROMACHI (1333–1568), AND MOMOYAMA (1568–1600) PERIODS

Minamoto Yoritomo established an institution which was to last through numerous vicissitudes from 1192 to 1868. This was the *Bakufu,* or "tent-government," which superseded the civil bureaucracy of the Heian period. Yoritomo reigned under the title *Shôgun,* or General-in-Chief. A man of the field and the provinces, Yoritomo founded his new military capital at Kamakura, far to the east of Kyoto, near the site of modern Tokyo. He was in theory a military officer of the Crown, but for the most part he spared himself the trouble of consulting the Throne on matters of state policy. The Bakufu controlled each of the provinces through a constable loyal to Yoritomo. Knights newly confirmed by Yoritomo were the landholders in this system and were largely independent but for the defensive obligations they owed the Bakufu. The laws promulgated by the new government at Kamakura were nothing more than an extension on a national scale of the clan law of the Minamoto family. It did not supplant the civil government but supplemented it; emperor, ministers, and civil bureaucrats—even the hereditary Fujiwara regency—continued to exist in Kyoto, but there the titles were increasingly empty and those who held them increasingly powerless.

The centralized military dictatorship of Kamakura was

tested in 1274 and 1281 by Japan's only historic invasions from abroad, by the Mongols under Kublai Khan. Though the Khans had built an empire stretching from China across central Asia to Lithuania, they failed to conquer Japan, due to a fortunate conjunction of Japanese prowess at arms and a typhoon in the Strait of Tsushima (the now legendary *kami-kaze,* or "divine wind"), which destroyed the second invading fleet. Though the victory assured Japan her independence, it foretold the collapse of the national unity that the Bakufu had purchased at so great a cost of arms. The cost of outfitting the defensive forces ruined the Bakufu financially but, more important, it encouraged independence in the outside lords, who were then in a position to contend for military supremacy.

A new dynasty of shoguns, the Ashikaga, provided fifteen rulers from 1338 until late in the sixteenth century, but most of them failed in the attempt to give the nation unified, secure government. Dissident military families fought the shoguns and one another continuously for control of territory. Rarely were more than the central provinces under the shogun's control. For many years in the fourteenth century an Ashikaga shogun held court in Kyoto with an emperor of his own sponsorship, while a rival emperor commanded the allegiance of other military families from a fortress-court fifty miles to the south at Yoshino. Warfare was intermittent during the entire period and after about 1470 was continuous throughout the country.

Trade relations with the Continent, which had languished in the long period after the first fruitful contacts, flourished again in the fifteenth and sixteenth centuries. Encouraged by the central government, Japanese *daimyō,* or feudal lords, traded with China and southeast Asia (their men sometimes in the role of pirates); they established a network of maritime influence of much importance to the history of oriental commerce.

In 1542 Portuguese traders landed in Kyushu and were followed in the next few years by Portuguese and Spanish missionaries who set out to convert Japan to Christianity. By the early seventeenth century, there were about 300,000 Japanese Christians; yet, for the most part, the effect of early Western contacts on Japan was not religious but military and political. When it appeared that Western nations had political designs on Eastern peoples, the Japanese nobles grew cautious in their attitude toward them. They gladly accepted Western improvements in arms and defense—musket design and castle architecture, for example—and were willing in some instances to Christianize their subjects in the hope of foreign military alliance against domestic enemies. They came to mistrust, then to reject, Christianity when they realized it might be a predecessor to subversion and conquest.

These unsettled times made military prowess more important than ancestry as a measure of social prestige. Scions of old aristocracy lost lands and status, whereas brave upstarts found themselves masters of provinces. The new maritime commerce and the need for permanent, expensive fortifications gave birth to cities, where a new social class of merchants dealing in coin and credit was to displace the simple agricultural and barter economy of older times.

Between 1565 and 1600, three military men led the reunification of Japan. The first of them, the minor territorial lord Oda Nobunaga, conquered many of the provinces of central Japan and broke the power, then formidable, of the large Buddhist monasteries. On his murder in 1582, his forces and lands fell to his foremost general, a remarkable soldier of peasant stock named Hideyoshi, who conquered or allied with the states of western Japan. From his new castle at Osaka he reigned as Prime Minister and Civil Dictator, titles which none but aristocrats had ever assumed. The nation unified and pacified, Hideyoshi sought a means of keeping his country's vast soldiery from thoughts of rebellion. An abortive invasion of Korea (with the conquest of China its eventual aim) was the result— Japan's only overseas war between the seventh and nineteenth centuries. Hideyoshi died in 1598 while Japanese troops were still in Korea. His greatest general and successor was Tokugawa Ieyasu, who, unlike Hideyoshi, was of aristocratic stock but, like him, was a self-made man.

THE TOKUGAWA PERIOD (1600–1868)

Tokugawa Ieyasu's problem in 1598 was to reinforce Hideyoshi's precarious military union with an efficient administrative system and the strength of law. In 1603 he had himself named hereditary Shogun. Political stability in monarchical Japan demanded a dynasty, and Ieyasu founded the line which was to govern until 1868.

Europeans in Japan labored under increasing difficulties under Hideyoshi and Ieyasu. Fear of Catholic conquest prompted Hideyoshi in 1587 to ban all missionaries from Japan. Proscription of Christianity after 1600 eventuated in bloody persecution of the European missionaries and their Japanese converts; and finally in 1637 a full-scale rebellion at the western

Kyushu outpost of Shimabara, in which 37,000 die-hard Japanese Christians were killed by the Shogun's armies, virtually did away with Christianity as an organized religion in Japan. In 1624 the third Tokugawa Shogun had expelled all Spaniards from Japan. By 1640 decrees were in force which excluded all Europeans from Japan as a whole, forbade Japanese from traveling abroad, and limited merchant vessels to a tonnage insufficient for overseas navigation. One small window was left open to foreign trade—and foreign cultural influence. Chinese and Dutch merchants were allowed to trade with official Japanese middlemen at Nagasaki. With a few exceptions the Dutch here provided Japan's only lawful contact with Europe for over two hundred years.

The peace and security that the Tokugawa shoguns gave Japan for two and a half centuries depended on a complex balance of forces—political, military, and economic. The shogun held certain lands outright (including his military capital at Edo, now Tokyo, and the commercial cities of Osaka and Nagasaki) or entrusted them to relatives or direct hereditary vassals (*fudai daimyô*). The "outside lords" (*tozama daimyô*), who submitted to Tokugawa rule at sword's point after 1600, were rendered harmless by isolating them in areas outside the central provinces and by severe restrictions on alliances among them. The system was in effect a close alliance of military states independent of the Bakufu in many of their internal affairs but strictly controlled by it in their relations with one another. Another source of national unity was the vague influence of the powerless emperor and his effete court at Kyoto, under the constant surveillance of a shogunal deputy.

All daimyo were allotted fiefs of land assessed in terms of

annual rice yield. The daimyo in turn paid their samurai (the
military, professional, and official class) fixed incomes reckoned
in terms of rice. Taxation was exacted from the peasantry in
food crops and exchange was to a large extent in the form of
barter. Yet Tokugawa economy was increasingly one of agri-
culture-plus-commerce, and the commercial wealth of the growing cities steadily tended to upset the purely agricultural economy that existed in theory. Economically the history of Japan
in the Tokugawa period is the story of the rising merchant
class's acquisition of more and more of the wealth of the gov-
erning classes, daimyo and samurai. With wealth came a distinctive city culture fostered by the merchant classes. Wealthy
commoners began to buy or marry their way into the samurai
class and in the process produced a new aristocracy partly of inheritance from the feudal nobility and partly of wealth.

The lot of the peasantry in the Tokugawa period was never
easy; in years of poor crops or times of disaster from fires,
floods, or earthquakes, it was bleak indeed. Agrarian revolts
were numerous, but they were minor uprisings, many blood-
less, to redress specific grievances in local areas rather than
against the Bakufu itself. The authorities had little to fear from
popular revolution. As the economy expanded in these years of
peace through the seventeenth and eighteenth centuries, the
standard of living increased somewhat, though possibilities in
that direction were naturally limited by the frozen economy of
a nation locked against foreign trade.

Two revolutionary developments of the nineteenth century
started the transformation of Japan into a modern nation. By
the first of them she reopened her harbors to foreign ships, encouraged her citizens to learn from the West, and began her

amazingly rapid rise to the status of a world power. By the second, she abolished feudalism and the system of dual government, shogunal and imperial, which had lasted for nearly seven hundred years. Forces inside and outside Japan effected these changes. Dissatisfaction against the shogun's authority was growing in many classes of society in the early part of the century and a few rebels looked forward to the restitution of the ancient Imperial House to supremacy as an instrument of state, not merely an ornamental symbol of national continuity. Certain *tozama daimyô,* notably the most powerful of those in western Japan, in Chôshû (western Honshu), and Satsuma (southern Kyushu), had wealth and military power rivaling that of the Bakufu and in coalition might hope to overthrow it. Scholars chafed under the seclusion edicts, which had been relaxed somewhat in 1720 to permit the introduction of European scientific and medical information to Japan, a step which only whetted the appetite for still more knowledge from the West.

After 1825 a series of attempts by Western powers to force an end to seclusion had as objectives guarantees of the care and safe return of shipwrecked sailors, provision of fueling ports, and the exploitation of a new field for commercial and missionary activity. It culminated in the successful Perry mission of 1853. Commodore Matthew Calbraith Perry obtained on behalf of the United States a shipwreck convention and also exacted from the Bakufu a promise to open diplomatic negotiations in the near future. America's first envoy, Townsend Harris, arrived in 1856 and two years later negotiated the treaty that formally opened Japan to relations with the West. Similar treaties with European powers followed shortly thereafter.

Reaction by the Bakufu's conservative enemies was instantaneous. Outrages against the hated foreigners increased. When an Englishman was murdered outside the new foreign port of Yokohama by samurai in the entourage of the daimyo of Satsuma, the British retaliated by bombarding the fief's capital of Kagoshima. The foreign supremacy of arms thus evidenced did not noticeably mollify Satsuma's hostility to trade (which one must remember was to be on terms imposed by the foreigners), but it did waken Japan to the necessity of strengthening national defenses if foreign demands were to be resisted. The battle cry of the dissidents at this time was, "Revere the Emperor; expel the barbarians." The prestige of the Imperial Court was called to aid in the crisis by the Shogun himself, who feared to assume sole responsibility for the revolutionary decisions he felt he must make. In 1865 the Throne acceded to the Shogun's request that additional ports be opened to foreign trade, but the Shogun had lost much prestige merely by making the request. At last a Shogun friendly to the Imperial cause took office and in 1867 abdicated to a new civilian government responsible to the Emperor alone.

THE MEIJI PERIOD

The Revolution of 1868 was a "restoration" to power of the Imperial dynasty, then embodied in a fifteen-year-old boy whose reign name (1868–1912) was Meiji. The Charter Oath pronounced by the Emperor at his removal to the Shogun's capital, then renamed Tokyo, was a hopefully liberal document calling for freedom of occupation, abolition of worn-out laws and customs, and deliberative assemblies representing "public opinion." The era was one of modernization of most phases of the national life. The government accomplished industrialization and achieved military preparedness with great speed and efficiency, but this entailed an inevitable sacrifice of the liberalism voiced in the Charter Oath. The Restoration leaders were for the most part young samurai of the great western fiefs plus a few bluebloods of the Kyoto nobility and former functionaries of the Bakufu. These men became a self-perpetuating oligarchy far more influential in the Meiji government than the Emperor himself. Some of the more important of them are mentioned here.

Iwakura Tomomi, Kido Kôin, Ôkubo Toshimichi, and Itô Hirobumi, in a series of policy decisions of the early seventies, set the national course for internal reforms, industrialization, and the establishment of a strong, centralized state.

Saigô Takamori, a model of samurai loyalty and courage, opposed them in favor of an aggressive foreign and military policy.

Yamagata Aritomo, founder of the modern Japanese Army, was in some ways most powerful of all the oligarchs. He introduced conscription, patterned the Army on the German model (after German victory in the Franco-Prussian War), and worked for fifty years to make Japan a world power and the Army a formidable instrument of state within it.

Whatever their differences, these men were united in their conviction that they alone had the necessary experience and responsibility to direct the affairs of state. All of them but the court noble Iwakura were samurai of Chôshû or Satsuma and made of those clans a virtual aristocracy within an aristocracy.

Itagaki Taisuke of Tosa and Ôkuma Shigenobu of Hizen

were the most eminent of this clique's opponents through the 1870's and 1880's. Their weapons were two European institutions that might in time break the power of the Council of State: parliamentary government and the political party. For whatever personal motives, these two men were foremost of the founders of Japanese liberalism.

The government abolished feudalism between 1869 and 1876. Daimyo surrendered their fiefs to the Throne, local administrative units were established subordinate to the central government, and the samurai were reduced from being hereditary arms-bearers and pensioners to the status of commoners. Resentment among the more conservative samurai, particularly those of Satsuma who were attracted by the forceful personality of Saigô Takamori, culminated in a rebellion against the government forces. The victory in 1877 of Yamagata's efficient army—including conscripts from the former commoner classes —over Saigô's aristocrats destroyed more of the past perhaps than had the Restoration itself.

Some of the oligarchs, Ôkubo and Itô among them, realized that parliamentary government was a feature of the strongest Western powers and thought it an eventual goal for Japan if she were to become fully modernized. On the other hand, they resented any diminution of personal power and resisted every attempt to broaden the base of government. Repression of parliamentary sentiment flared up as late as 1878, after Ôkubo was assassinated for his conservatism. Itagaki and Ôkuma, the former safely outside the government and the latter about to leave it, forced the hand of the clan oligarchs by exposing their graft and corruption and obtained the promise of a National Diet to be convened nine years later (1890). With elec-

tions in the offing, Japan's first political parties made their
appearance. Itagaki's Liberal Party (Jiyû-tô) catered to the
farmer and small-propertied classes, whereas Ôkuma's Progressives (Kaishin-tô) favored the economic and intellectual
upper classes. The government "ins" countered ineffectually
with a party of their own, the Imperial Government Party
(Teisei-tô), Imperial rule to these men meaning their own
continuance in power. Itô Hirobumi made a trip to Europe to
study existing parliaments. Theoretically free to choose between an oligarchic German or liberal English model, Itô decided on the German as better suited to Japan's needs and to
preserving imperial rule. Hence the Prussian-style cabinet
which replaced the Council of State in 1885 was a powerful and
self-perpetuating executive body of clan bureaucrats. A constitution, promulgated in 1889, appeased further liberal demands, but in effect it merely confirmed continued rule of
the oligarchy. The National Diet of 1890 was elected by a
limited body of voters; its powers were severely restricted by
executive prerogatives of the cabinet.

Though the adoption of Western parliamentarianism failed
to produce truly liberal political institutions, Japanese economic
modernization on Western lines was phenomenally successful.
Enterprising merchants and financiers started that process of
concentration of capital which produced the "financial clique"
(*zaibatsu*) in later years. Zaibatsu firms organized an electric
power system and built the great textile and coal industries.
The demand for native-controlled shipping produced the O.S.K.
(Osaka Shôsen Kaisha) and N.Y.K. (Nippon Yûsen Kaisha)
lines, both in operation by 1885. The government educated the
public in the operations of finance capital from 1870 on and

encouraged the establishment of banks, insurance companies, and commodities exchanges. In 1882 Finance Minister Matsukata Masayoshi led the foundation of a central banking agency, The Bank of Japan (modeled after the Bank of Belgium), with powers to issue convertible bank notes, to regulate the national currency and foreign exchange of specie and bullion, and to furnish capital to banks and businesses.

As military preparedness was the principal aim of industrialization, munitions plants, heavy industries, and communications facilities were the first to be established. Many goods for domestic consumption continued to be produced under the ancient cottage industry system, though within a few decades the factory system introduced for the sake of producing arms was turning out civilian goods as well.

The Ministry of Education, organized in 1871, concentrated on a program of elementary education to eradicate illiteracy and train a loyal populace in the duties of citizenship. Tokyo University (1877) was the first of the national schools that were to train most of Japan's succeeding civil servants and set the standards for the education of future generations of business and professional leaders. A westernized press served the government's purposes in keeping the public aware of its new responsibilities, but it also offered liberals and dissenters some freedom of expression on all sorts of matters. The proscription of Christianity had been removed in 1873, and the missionary movement, Catholic and Protestant, proceeded apace from that time. Interest in Western religion and philosophy typified the westernizing spirit of the new age.

In the social sphere, the government abolished the samurai and *eta* classes, the latter having been limited for centuries to menial or humiliating occupations and an outcast social status. Women's rights lagged behind other social reforms, but schools for women were established in the seventies and eighties, and women gained legal rights to head households and initiate divorce actions.

FOREIGN RELATIONS (1868–1920)

Japanese diplomacy between 1870 and the early nineties was aimed at gaining the diplomatic equality with foreign nations that extraterritoriality, restrictions on tariff autonomy, and most-favored-nation clauses of the early Western treaties specifically denied her. The government set up a Foreign Ministry in 1869 and sent emissaries abroad in 1872 which urged treaty revision by the powers, but decided not to press the matter while Japan was militarily defenseless. The treaty by which Russia recognized the Japanese right to the Kuriles (1875) and China's *de facto* recognition of Japanese sovereignty in the Ryukyus (1881–95) were diplomatic triumphs that started Japan on her way to wide-scale territorial expansion. Of greater importance were the negotiations over Japan's diplomatic rights in Korea. The Chinese Empire considered Korea a tributary state, whereas Japan claimed she was independent. Japan gained full diplomatic and postal rights in Korea in 1880, but a civil dispute in that country brought China and Japan into another disagreement on the issue of Korean independence. The settlement that Itô Hirobumi obtained from the Chinese Minister Li Hung-Chang (Li-Ito Convention, 1885) provided that neither country could dispatch troops to Korea without previously notifying the other. The real issue in the case was which of the countries was to dominate Korea. The Convention postponed a decision, allowing Japan to concentrate on treaty revision. Great Britain announced the intention of giving up her extraterritorial rights whenever Japan should reform her judicial system to conform to Western standards. Further negotiations led to treaties (1894–99) granting full judicial sovereignty, while full tariff autonomy came with the U.S.–Japanese Treaty of Commerce and Navigation of 1911.

The Sino-Japanese War of 1894–95 confirmed Japan's position as a Far Eastern power, and the Russo-Japanese War of 1904–5 made her a world power. Both conflicts concerned foreign influence in Korea and Manchuria. The former gained for Japan Western admiration of her progress; it gave her Formosa and the Pescadores; it won for her several commercial advantages in China. The peace treaty originally granted Japan the Liaotung Peninsula (on the Manchurian coast), but the so-called Triple Intervention of Russia, France, and Germany forced her to give up this prize. (Popular rancor in Japan at this move was of lasting effect in the modification of future foreign policy.) China's antiforeign Boxer Uprising of 1900 gave Japan an opportunity to confirm her status as a power when the others requested that she send a large share of the troops to quell it, but it worked also to Russia's advantage by deflecting the attention of the powers from her simultaneous occupation of Manchuria. The Anglo-Japanese Alliance of 1902 was in recognition of the threat which European, particularly Russian, designs on Chinese and Korean territorial integrity held for the peace of the Far East. Backed by English friendship, Japan could undertake a war with Russia without fear of intervention by a third power. Japanese victory over Russia (1905)

assured her "paramount political, military, and economic interests" in Korea, secured in southern Manchuria the special
railroad and commercial rights which had been Russia's, and
gave her southern Sakhalin. The Japanese public were dis-
appointed that the Treaty of Portsmouth did not grant still
more concessions, but Japan's world position was assured by it.

As a result, Japanese-American relations became of greater
moment. Two principal points were at issue: (1) commercial
rivalry in China and (2) Japanese immigration to America.
Proximity plus the 1905 concessions gave Japan advantages in
the China trade. Korea was virtually a Japanese colony after
1907, actually so after 1910. The Root-Takahira agreement of
1908 alleviated tension by guaranteeing mutual respect of the
other nation's rights and possessions in the Far East. Meanwhile, feelings against Japanese immigrants in America's western states mounted. Cheap oriental labor was thought to be a
threat to the standard of living of American laborers. The
Hearst papers and other elements of the California press ag-
gravated the situation, demanding exclusion of Orientals.
There was talk of war over the issue, but in 1908 the Japanese
themselves relieved the tension by the so-called Gentlemen's
Agreement, whereby Japan refused passports to laborers and
their families wishing to emigrate to the United States, in return for which the American government was not to affront
the national pride by prohibiting Japanese immigration altogether. The American Immigration Law of 1924 was a breach
of the Gentlemen's Agreement and created much ill will toward
America in Japan.

Japan joined the Allied side in the First World War in
August, 1914. Her military and naval forces occupied Kiaochow

and Tsingtao, the German concession on the China coast, and Germany's Pacific possessions and, by the end of the war, was policing the Indian Ocean from Australia to South Africa. Japan took advantage of the war to issue demands to China (the Twenty-one Demands) aimed at establishing for Japan a dominant economic and political position on the Continent. Japanese aims at the Versailles Conference were limited primarily to confirmation of her possession of the former German concession in China and cession of Germany's Pacific possessions north of the equator (the Carolines, Marianas, and Marshalls). Both were granted. The war years had been a time of unprecedented prosperity for Japanese business, and the nation emerged as one of the Big Five world powers. Early in 1918, before the end of the war, Japan joined the United States and other Allies in an expedition to Siberia with the aim of putting down the Bolsheviks. American troops withdrew in 1920, but the Japanese remained until 1922, obviously with the objective of capitalizing on the Russian crisis to strengthen Japan's own continental position. By the Treaty of Versailles, Japan had a permanent seat on the Council of the League of Nations. Chinese opposition to Japan's leasehold in Shantung eventually led to relinquishment of the concession to Chinese sovereignty, though Japan retained a lien on the railways and a Japanese traffic manager.

In an attempt to control economic development of China through an international body and hence forestall further spheres of influence or territorial concessions to individual nations, the United States proposed at the Versailles Conference the establishment of a financial consortium, or international loan-making body. Japan at first refused to participate in it but agreed later when assurances were given that her privileges in Manchuria would not be threatened.

Political history entered a new phase after the convening of the first Diet in 1890. The clan oligarchs continued to dominate the cabinet and further strengthened their position through two extraparliamentary bodies of a conservative nature. The first of these, the *genrô,* or elder statesmen, consisted of past servants of the Imperial cause who came with advancing age to enjoy the special trust of the Emperor and government. The second body, the Privy Council, came into being in 1888 to approve the new Constitution before its promulgation. It had powers of review and veto of legislation as well as advisory functions. The political parties continued to work for strengthening of representative government.

For a decade or so, advocates of party government vied for control with the supporters of oligarchic control. For the first few years, elder statesmen firmly entrenched in the oligarchic cabinet succeeded one another as prime minister—Yamagata, Matsukata, Itô, Matsukata, Itô. Then for a few months in 1898 the newly formed Constitutional Party (Kensei-tô) formed a cabinet under the pioneers of liberalism, Itagaki and Ôkuma. The Kensei-tô, like succeeding parties, was hardly more than a coalition of individuals dissatisfied with oligarchic rule, and the cabinet it formed collapsed soon after from internal dissensions. Its successor was another government of clan bureaucrats under Yamagata. The Imperial Ordinance of 1900, which this cabinet promulgated, was in later years to do more perhaps than any other single measure to impede the progress of popular or representative government in Japan. The Ordinance remained in effect until after the Second World War and provided that only top-ranking officers of the armed services might hold the posts of War and Navy ministers. Since the services themselves might withdraw their ministers or refuse to recommend new ones, the provision gave them an absolute veto power over the civilian government. An upsurge of chauvinism at the time of the Russo-Japanese War further handicapped truly liberal government. A variety of factions formed succeeding cabinets until the post–First World War governments formed on the basis of Diet composition once more gave promise of party government responsive to the will of the electorate.

The socialist movement in Japan up to the First World War was almost completely dissociated from the constitutional or parliamentary struggle here outlined. Though Itagaki's Liberal Party of the early eighties had social reform aims, the foundations of Japanese radicalism were in the Oriental Socialist Party founded in 1882 and in various labor associations of the 1890's. A political party of 1901 was suppressed by the government, while the pacifist leanings of socialist groups during the Russo-Japanese War further roused the government against radical movements as a whole. In 1910 an alleged plot by the anarchist Kôtoku Denjirô to assassinate the Emperor resulted in violent suppression of all left-wing organizations, most of which were incomparably more moderate than Kôtoku's anarchists. The incident led to almost complete extirpation of the socialist movement in Japan for about a decade. Fear of radicalism continued to be a force in Japanese politics and was used

by conservatives to thwart many a move toward democracy in
the twenties and thirties.

EXPANSION AFTER THE FIRST WORLD WAR

For a few years after the First World War it appeared that
militarism and the repression of liberalism were on the way
out. The Hara Cabinet of 1918 was the first to be headed by a
member of the House of Representatives. Party pluralities in
the House determined the composition of the cabinet. Inter-
nationally, Japan appeared willing to cooperate with the
League of Nations and abandon her policy of aggression
toward Asia. At the Washington Conference of 1922 she agreed
to withdraw from the Anglo-Japanese Alliance, vacate Shantung and Siberia, and reduce naval armaments. In the same
year, however, conservatives on the Emperor's advisory coun-
cils took direct action to reverse this trend by appointing the
first of a series of military men to form cabinets. The American
Immigration Act of 1924 embittered the nation and confirmed
the existing contempt of its leaders for the sanctity of international agreements. The depletion of Japanese credit due to
a temporary collapse in the silk market and overvaluation of
the yen contributed to general economic instability, already of
serious proportions when the world-wide crash of 1929 struck.
The Premier at the time, Hamaguchi Yûkô, by advocating
Japanese participation in the London Naval Treaty of 1930,
aroused the hatred of the militarists. In September, 1931, a
"Manchurian clique" in the Army proceeded independently of
the civilian government to instigate the first of a series of "in-

cidents" designed ostensibly to protect Japanese railway interests in Manchuria, but actually aimed at making Manchuria a colony under the sole control of the Army. Manchuria, which had never been under the control of the central government of the Chinese Nationalists, was declared the independent country of Manchoukuo (1932) but was actually a Japanese possession in which the Army tested its plans for a war-directed, controlled economy. Huge government-financed businesses and industries aroused the envy of the Japanese zaibatsu, many of whose members were thereby persuaded to accept managerial positions in the continental development companies.

Assassination of government leaders had been an effective way for dissatified elements to make their objections known since before the Restoration. After the murder of Prime Minister Inukai in 1932, this threat hung over any official who opposed the designs of the militarists. Too often the government failed to punish assassins, most of whom were visibly sincere in the "patriotic" motives for their acts. A full-scale coup d'état by young Army extremists in February, 1936, followed a defeat for the ultranationalists at the polls. Three senior ministers among the moderates were killed and the rest of the government, which included some moderates, was terrorized into submission to the demands of the extremists.

Meanwhile, the Army's continental policy had become more and more aggressive. Japan withdrew from the League of Nations in 1933 when the latter threatened sanctions for the Manchurian Incident. The North Chinese province of Jehol was annexed to Manchoukuo in the same year. In 1935 the "Autonomous" Council of East Hopei brought more North Chinese territory under Japanese military control. A clash between

Japanese and Chinese troops at Marco Polo Bridge near Peking in July, 1937, finally launched open war between Japan and the Nationalist government of Chiang Kai-shek. Local Japanese military authorities in China commenced all-out aerial and ground attacks, and the Tokyo government was forced to back them by dispatching troops. Immediate protests by the United States and the League of Nations against this aggression were useless. Japanese troops soon occupied the China coast south to the Yangtze River. The unprovoked attack (December, 1937) on the U.S. gunboat *Panay* in the river above Nanking created serious international tension, threatenening war between the two countries, until expression of regret by the Japanese government and public restored calm. The National Mobilization Law of 1938 and establishment of a puppet government in occupied China brought the nation several steps closer to domination by its expansionist and repressive militarists.

By diverting British and French attention from the Far East, the outbreak of the Second World War gave Japan further opportunities for aggression. Late in 1940, Japan was granted military privileges in Indo-China by the Vichy government. The three-power pact of that time with Germany and Italy gave Japan Axis blessing for any acts she might undertake to complete the conquest of the entire Far East. An economic and political empire centered in Tokyo and embracing all of East Asia (the Greater East Asia Co-Prosperity Sphere) became the dream of Japanese leaders. The aim could be accomplished short of war only if the Axis partnership were maintained at the same time the United States and the Soviet Union remained neutral. Foreign Minister Matsuoka Yôsuke endeav-

ored through 1941 to appease all sides and to reach an agreement with the Chinese Nationalists, but he made countenance
of further aggression a requisite to amity and was hence unsuc-
cessful in appeasing the Western democracies. General Tôjô
Hideki became Premier in October of that year and totalitarian
military dictatorship was in control. Eight weeks later the
attacks on Pearl Harbor and Manila proclaimed the failure of
diplomacy as Japan turned the United States from unfriendly
neutral to active belligerent in the Second World War.

Japanese leaders relied on American lack of preparedness and
the unwillingness of the American people to make necessary
sacrifices to assure victory. If the expected German victory in
Europe had occurred, Japan might have been able to negotiate
a peace with America from a position of great strength in Asia.
Admiral Yamamoto's oft-misquoted remark that Japan—to win
—would have to dictate peace terms in the White House was
an expression of caution from a moderate Navy man chary of
Japan's ability to achieve more than partial victory over the
United States. When eventual defeat should have been apparent
to the government, extremists in the Army still held out for a
miracle that never materialized. The war dragged on two or
more years after the tide turned against Japan. Atomic bomb-
ing of Hiroshima and Nagasaki in August, 1945, was for the
purpose not of assuring victory for the Allies, which was certain anyway, but of avoiding the costly invasion of the Japanese islands which the Japanese Army seemed determined to
let happen. Russia entered the war the same week and forced
troops in Manchuria to capitulate. A cabinet decision, aided
by direct intervention of the Emperor, brought hostilities to an
end on August 14, 1945.

Surrender terms were formulated by heads of state of the United States, England, and China at Potsdam in July, 1945, and called for surrender of troops and arms, demobilization, and submission to Allied occupation (the United States to be the chief occupying power for the Allies). General Douglas MacArthur, who had been wartime Commander of Allied Forces in the Southwest Pacific, was named Supreme Commander for the Allied Powers (SCAP). The extent of Japan's defeat may be judged by the statistics: nearly 1,500,000 troops and civilians killed; 30 percent of the urban population homeless; 40 percent of the urban area leveled; industry reduced to 33 percent of its 1936–37 productive capacity. Clearly, reconstruction and rehabilitation were the first problems to be faced. Punishment of war criminals; removal of militarists and their accomplices from positions of responsibility in government, business, and professions; and tutelage of the nation in the mechanics of democratic self-government were stated to be the basic aims of the occupation.

The first phase of the occupation lasted until about 1948, when the initial aims seemed on their way to accomplishment. An elaborate occupation government consisting of sections for the administration of political, economic, and educational policies took its orders from the Supreme Commander and relayed them to the Japanese government. A new Constitution set the pattern for a constitutional monarchy with parliamentary control similar to that in Britain and outlawed war as an instrument of national policy. A land reform program redistributed land in the hands of absentee owners to the farmers who worked it. Military government teams in the prefectures supervised the reorganization of local governments, which were to have greater independence than before. Some capital equipment in the possession of the government was distributed as reparation to Asian victims of Japanese aggression. Over four thousand war criminals were punished and thousands more of the nation's former leaders were barred from public office. The educational system was thoroughly reformed, giving greater autonomy to local school boards and outlawing the teaching of militant nationalism. These policies were for the most part conceived and implemented by American authorities, though the British Commonwealth provided occupying troops for some areas, and all the wartime Allies nominally supervised the occupation through the Far Eastern Commission of eleven members (later thirteen) in Washington and the Allied Council of four members in Tokyo.

The first postwar elections, in April, 1946, gave the two major conservative parties, the Liberals and the Progressives, a plurality in the House of Representatives and made the Liberal leader, Yoshida Shigeru, Prime Minister. The Communist Party, newly permitted to run candidates, did more poorly than expected, with only 3.8 percent of the popular vote for the House. Elections in April, 1947, under the new laws showed an increase of Socialist strength and gave the premiership to the Socialist leader, Katayama Tetsu. A profusion of political parties prevented any one of them from forming a majority cabinet; the government was a coalition including the moderate Democrats and members of the People's Cooperative Party. Internal cabinet shifts made the Democrat Ashida Hitoshi Prime Minister, but the withdrawal of the Socialists and charges of corruption in the government forced general elections in January, 1949. Yoshida Shigeru again became

Prime Minister and remained so for the rest of the occupation.

Early in the occupation international events began to force American aims in Japan into a radically different direction from that envisaged during the war. Demobilization and demilitarization had been rapid, and democratization, so far as could be determined at the time, had been accomplished to an amazing degree. From 1947 on the American government attempted to bring the occupation to a close through a peace treaty but encountered opposition from the Soviet Union, which had as great a stake in the failure of the Allied reforms as the United States had in their success. Speedy economic rehabilitation for Japan became the major American objective, whereas ironically Japan's defenselessness seemed only to work to the advantage of the Communists. Communist strength at the polls had never been a serious threat, but the hard-core Communist minority in Japan could be counted on to capitalize on the dissatisfactions a long occupation would inevitably entail.

After the outbreak of the Korean War in June, 1950, the necessity of launching the United Nations offensive from Japanese soil made Japan's nonsovereign status an increasing embarrassment. In 1951 it was decided to forego the advantages of a joint peace by all the Second World War belligerents, and in September of that year forty-eight nations signed a peace treaty with Japan, Russia abstaining. A security pact with the United States signed at the same time assured Japan of at least temporary defenses without causing her to abandon her constitutional position against the maintenance of armed forces. A national police reserve of 75,000 men had been created in 1950 to relieve some of America's defense burden. By mid-1955 it had grown to a full-fledged self-defense force and comprised six land divisions of 130,000 uniformed troops, a 16,000-man navy with 69,000 tons of vessels built or under construction, and a 6,700-man air force with 142 planes.

Late in 1954 disaffection among members of his own party forced Yoshida out as leader of the Liberals and brought an end to his long premiership. Since the elections of February, 1955, the majority of the Diet's membership has continued to be of a fundamentally conservative cast, but the policies of subsequent Prime Ministers Hatoyama Ichirô, Ishibashi Tanzan, and Kishi Nobusuke have included not only continuance of Japan's friendship with the Western nations but also resumption of normal relations with the Soviet Union and Communist China.

Domestic policies of recent cabinets have likewise shown a tendency to reverse the course set by American occupation reforms. There has, for example, been a certain amount of recentralization of governmental affairs, and more threatens to follow.

READINGS

Borton, Hugh. *Japan's Modern Century*. New York, Ronald Press, 1955.

Reischauer, Edwin O. *Japan; Past and Present*. 2nd ed., revised and enlarged. New York, Alfred A. Knopf, 1953.

Sansom, George Bailey. *Japan; a Short Cultural History*. Rev. ed. New York, Appleton-Century, 1944.

———— *The Western World and Japan; a Study in the Interaction of European and Asiatic Cultures*. New York, Alfred A. Knopf, 1950.

Tiedemann, Arthur. *Modern Japan, a Brief History*. Princeton, D. Van Nostrand Co., 1955.

GOVERNMENT

The present form of government in Japan dates only from the Constitution of 1947, but many of its features can be traced to much earlier times. Japan's progress toward constitutional democracy can best be understood against the background of the institutions and habits she had inherited from before the war.

GENERAL FEATURES OF PREWAR GOVERNMENT

Prewar Japan was in theory an absolute monarchy. The emperor might, if he chose, declare all the existing laws null and void or declare war or replace all the government officials and functionaries with others more to his liking. The Constitution of 1889 was his "gift" to the people. It outlined the forms under which the actual government operated, but it in no way diminished the supreme authority outside the law which the emperor held by virtue of his "divine" descent. In practice, of course, no emperor ever held such unreserved power. The very sanctity of the position made it unfitting for the sovereign to trouble himself with affairs of practical politics. The elaborate machinery of government consisted of fully competent ministers and bureaucrats whose theoretical role was either to "advise" the emperor or to carry out his commands.

With the single reservation that the emperor *could if he wished* rule with unbridled authority, the government need not have been despotic in practice. Throughout the Meiji and Taishô periods (1868–1926) there was much agitation for parliamentary rule in which the cabinet should be directly responsible to the will of the electorate. Actually, such a state of affairs never came about, primarily because Japan's educated leadership thought in terms of oligarchy and resisted attempts to place government in the hands of the inexperienced masses.

The actual wielders of power varied from time to time in the seventy years before the outbreak of the Second World War. The Meiji Restoration had been led by a few young samurai of the great semi-independent feudal clans of western Japan. These men continued to lead the government in Meiji times. The Council of State until 1885, then all succeeding cabinets from that date until after the First World War, were dominated by members of this clan oligarchy or by their protégés. After 1900 the oligarchy began to be infiltrated increasingly by members of the military caste, for these men, whatever their origins, owed their positions to military organizers within the clan oligarchy such as Field Marshal Yamagata of Chôshû or Admiral Yamamoto of Satsuma. Even the more or less liberal opposition to the Chôshû-Satsuma oligarchy, men like Itagaki Taisuke and Ôkuma Shigenobu, were ex-samurai of other powerful western clans. After 1918 there was a tendency for cabinets to represent majority parties within the Diet, though these governments were powerless to prevent the independent action of extraparliamentary groups such as the Army. Military domination of the civilian government increased after the Manchurian Incident of 1931, giving rise to a new oligarchy of rightist extremists in the Army and Navy and their supporters among the business or bureaucrat classes.

The Imperial Diet had two houses, the House of Peers and the House of Representatives. The former consisted of members of the nobility, men of distinguished service to the state, and high taxpayers. Membership was by Imperial appointment or election by classes represented, and the body was as a consequence very conservative. The House of Representatives represented geographical districts. After 1925 all adult males enjoyed the right to elect its members. The Japanese lower house lacked the power of budgetary control that might have made it the most effective instrument of government, for a constitutional provision stipulated that in any case of Diet refusal to pass a government appropriation, the previous year's budget should simply remain in effect. In addition, the Imperial prerogative gave the oligarchy an absolute veto over all Diet legislation.

Administrative functions of government belonged to the ministries, manned by professional bureaucrats and headed by members of the cabinet. From time to time the latter was a body of majority party leaders from the House of Representatives, but more often its membership depended on the choice of another fundamentally conservative body, the Privy Council, whose members held lifetime appointments from the Emperor. Still another advisory organ wielded much authority in the first quarter of the twentieth century. This was the genro, or elder statesmen, an extraconstitutional body of Satsuma or Chôshû clansmen (Itô, Yamagata, Inoue, Matsukata, Ôyama, and Katsura) plus the court noble, Prince Saionji.

Political parties in prewar Japan were originally liberal in purpose, since they were combinations of politicians out of power who wished to break the oligarchy's control. Later the oligarchs themselves saw the advantages to be gained by working through party organizations. In no case were parties unified around principles or coherent plans of action; all were directed by strong leaders, and new parties frequently came into being through bolts by politicians dissatisfied with their old alliances. On the whole, party government was never effectively realized. Promises that the two leading parties of the twenties might evolve a truly bipartisan government were dashed by the economic unrest and militarism of the thirties. As one cause, the ruling classes could never entirely dissociate the notion of an opposition party from disloyalty to the country. Radical parties continued to exist even under strong repression. The Social Democratic Party of the mid-thirties even managed to win thirty-seven Diet seats in the 1937 elections, while radical rightist groups such as that of Kita Ikki gave spiritual support to the frankly fascist domestic program of the extreme militarists. The small and illegal Japan Communist Party, founded in 1922, remained active through most of the 1920's with the constant infusion of new blood from among Moscow-trained revolutionaries but was forced into underground quiescence by the militarist repressions of the late twenties and thirties.

The above description applies to the forms Japanese were used to before 1945. The system was monolithic in a sense unfamiliar to Americans, for there were no autonomous local governments in which to experiment with the liberal novelties of women's suffrage, initiative and referendum, or toleration of radicals. The drawbacks of the system are obvious: it tended to concentrate power in the hands of a few venerables and keep it there; it tended to repress all progress toward liberalism or democracy; most disastrous of all, it allowed unbridled control of the civilian government by the least moderate elements in the military. The strong points are not so easy to see from our point of view, but they might be said to have included stability and encouragement (in early Meiji) of rapid achievement of military and industrial strength. In addition, the system took into account the public's lack of political experience and satisfied such urges to absolutism as Japan's Confucian and Shinto tradition produced.

THE POSTWAR GOVERNMENT

Japan's present government rests on the foundation of the Constitution of 1947. This has been criticized as a wholly American document forced on an occupied country in no position to modify or reject it. To this it might be countered that Japan could probably have achieved a democratic constitution in no other way. Foremost of its innovations was the reduction of the emperor from absolute sovereign to mere symbol of state, who may not refuse the signature necessary to make Diet enactments into law. Accordingly, the new government was to be based on law before which all persons, even the emperor, were to be treated equally. The Constitution further provided for supremacy of the Diet as the legislative power, separation of powers—legislative, executive (the cabinet and ministries), and judicial (the courts)—and guarantees of popular liberties.

The Diet consists, as before, of two houses, but the House of Peers has been replaced by the wholly elected House of Councillors. The House of Representatives consists of 467 members elected from geographical districts. It is the stronger of the two

houses, particularly in fiscal and foreign affairs. The prime
minister and at least half of his cabinet must be chosen from its
membership. The House of Councillors, with a membership of
250, includes members elected from the nation at large. Its
powers are inferior to those of the lower house, which may kill
bills it passes and may pass bills over its veto. On the other
hand, the House of Representatives may be dissolved by the
cabinet, forcing new elections, while councillors are elected to
fixed terms of six years, and the upper house itself is not subject
to dissolution.

The cabinet remains the principal executive organ in the
government, much stronger than before, since the old Privy
Council has been abolished. The nineteen cabinet members
draft proposed legislation and submit it to the Diet, administer
the executive ministries, supervise foreign relations, draw up a
budget for Diet approval, and act on amnesties and commuta-
tions of punishment.

The twelve executive ministries are headed by cabinet members. Most of the ministries are carry-overs from the prewar
government. In keeping with the delegation of broad powers to
local governments, the old Home Ministry, which administered
the national police force and controlled prefectural assemblies,
has been abolished. The old Ministry of Justice, which was in
effect the judiciary arm of government, has been replaced by
another ministry, the Attorney General's office, entrusted with
the duties of a public prosecutor under an independent judiciary. Significant too is the innovation of a Ministry of Labor
to enforce Japan's liberalized labor legislation. The extensive
civil service, though largely employed by the ministries, is
under a separate authority independent of cabinet control.

The new judiciary system is an independent branch of government equal in authority to the Diet and cabinet, whose decisions are subject to judicial review, as in the American legal system. The system consists of a Supreme Court, eight regional higher courts, district courts in each of the prefectures, and a number of summary courts. Family courts to adjudicate domestic complaints attest to the diminution of the power of family heads, once almost absolute, and the substitution for it of equal rights under law for all members of a family. A curious feature of the judiciary system is the provision that judges be reapproved by the people in the general elections following their appointment by the cabinet and at specified intervals thereafter. If a majority of voters favor the removal of a judge already appointed, he must be replaced. Furthermore, judges of the Supreme Court must be "learned persons of experience," and a certain number of them must be legal experts of at least twenty years' professional standing. Police powers have been removed completely from the judiciary as one of the first legal reforms designed to prevent a recurrence of abuses resulting from concentration of legal power. As a deterrent to police brutality in criminal cases, confessions must be supported by other evidence.

No constitutional provision has been of more revolutionary impact than that forbidding armed forces and abolishing war "as an instrument of national policy." It was adopted in the hope that in the brave new postwar world it would be possible for a nation of Japan's strategic importance to remain the "Switzerland of the East," immune from attack because of her very defenselessness. In the succeeding cold war American policymakers soon realized that an impotent Japan would at best be a lasting burden on American defenses if she was to remain secure from communist aggression. Maintenance of United Nations troops in Japan during the Korean War in effect postponed the necessity of providing Japan permanent self-defense. A home defense force was instituted shortly before the conclusion of the peace treaty, but its existence poses a thorny constitutional problem. To date, the Constitution remains unamended, and most Japanese have expressed themselves at the polls as opposing immediate rearmament.

Local government in Japan has been returned to the localities themselves, but there is no assurance that it will stay there. Mayors and governors of municipalities and prefectures are now elected directly by the people, as are local school boards. Local governments control school affairs, may levy emergency taxes, and have certain legislative powers. The efficiency of the local governments, particularly in regard to school boards, has been severely questioned of late. Certainly many local officials have lacked experience in government. In 1954 police affairs were returned to the control of the central government.

POLITICAL PARTIES

Before the war Japan's two leading political parties were the Seiyûkai and Minsei-tô. With the revival of party government in the autumn of 1945, both reappeared to become the leading conservative parties, the former as the Liberal Party and the latter as the Progressive Party. Meanwhile, members of former proletarian parties organized the Japan Social Democratic Party, and the Communist Party came out of hiding with the return from exile or release from prison of its former leaders.

A profusion of minor parties ranged from right to left behind candidates of widely varying backgrounds and degrees of political experience. In the 1946 general elections, 267 parties entered candidates. An inevitable weeding out of most of the minor parties and splits or consolidations of the more vigorous of them have made for a gradual simplification of the party scene. Since late in 1955 there have been two main parties, which between them have filled all but a handful of seats in the lower house and three quarters of those in the upper house. Backgrounds, policies, and personalities of the major parties are as follows.

A. The Japan Socialist Party (Nihon Shakai-tô). Pre-occupation suppression of the socialist movement gave the Japanese left wing a cohesiveness under stress that it was not long to maintain after it was freed for political activity. Early solidarity of the Social Democratic Party (Shakai Minshu-tô) led to unexpected strength at the polls in April, 1947, followed by strong positions for the party in the two succeeding coalition cabinets under their own leader Katayama Tetsu, from May, 1947, until March, 1948, and under Prime Minister Ashida, a Progressive, until October, 1948. Yet there came to be fundamental differences between extremists and moderates within the party. In October, 1951, the two wings split. The immediate issue was Japanese ratification of a peace treaty in the drafting of which neither the Soviet Union nor China had participated. Right Wingers, though they opposed the U.S.-Japanese defense pact that accompanied the treaty, supported the treaty itself. This the Left Wing refused to do. The Right Wing took a firm stand against rearmament, but avoided commitment to outright anti-Americanism.

Meanwhile, Left-Wing Socialists maintained strict opposition to cooperation with the West in all phases of its struggle with world communism. It opposed active and passive aid to the South Korean cause during the Korean War and after the war favored complete withdrawal of foreign defense troops from Japanese soil. At the same time it staunchly resisted rearmament for Japan either with or without amendment of the Constitution. Such a program attracted some of Japan's neutralists, to whom commitment on either side of the cold war seemed ill-advised, but it also appealed to those committed on the side of communism who were not actually Communist Party members.

Relaxation of American-Soviet tension in 1955 had the effect of diminishing some of the issues between the two wings, and in October, 1955, they merged to form the Japan Socialist Party. Suzuki Mosaburô, leader of the Left Wing, became party chairman, while Right-Wing leader Asanuma Inejirô became chief secretary. Some disagreements still remain among factions of the party, though all of them agree on an anti-capitalistic program of domestic economy and a greater or lesser degree of opposition to the pro-American foreign program of the majority party. Socialists hold less than a third of the seats in the House of Representatives, but their program has powerful support among labor unions and in intellectual circles.

B. The Liberal-Democratic Party (Jiyû-Minshu-tô). Japan's present majority party is basically conservative and favors alliance with the West. It came into being in November, 1955, with the union of the Liberal and Democratic parties. The latter had consisted of the members of the old Progressive

Party plus dissidents from the Liberals. Postwar conservative factions exhibit at least one of the striking characteristics of their prewar counterparts: they unify not so much around articulated programs or policies as behind dominating politicians. Personality clashes among conservative leaders delayed formation of a united party until after reconciliation of the Left- and Right-Wing Socialists had made it a political necessity. These clashes have continued to plague the new party since its establishment. It remains to be seen whether the union will be stable.

In March, 1957, Kishi Nobusuke, who became Prime Minister on February 25, was made head of the party.

C. The Ryokufû-kai. In 1947 a group of House of Councillors members of generally conservative political philosophy formed a separate party known as the Ryokufû-kai, or "Green Breeze Society." Its importance to Japanese political life lies in the fact that its upper-house membership of thirty-one seats prevents either of the major parties from obtaining majority control in the House of Councillors. The Ryokufû-kai fared badly in the elections of July, 1956, and may be heading for extinction.

D. The Japan Communist Party (Nihon Kyôsan-tô). Communist strength in Japan cannot be gauged by its numerical strength in the Diet, which declined from a high of thirty-five representatives after the January, 1949, elections to its present figure of two members in the lower house and two in the upper. In terms of its discipline, its hidden external support by Russia and the international party organization, and its potential appeal in times of crisis to possible millions not now swayed by its program, the Japan Communist Party must be considered one of the major parties. Its avowed aims include immediate withdrawal of U.S. security forces, abrogation of the U.S.–Japanese defense pact, continued disarmament, and social reforms. Incorporation of Japan into the communist bloc of nations is an ultimate aim.

During the occupation years the party offered a program of so-called peaceful revolution, designed to build popular support and at the same time ward off the wrath of the occupying authorities that would have resulted from a more overtly revolutionary policy. In consequence, orders from Moscow in January, 1950, purged top Japanese party officials, replacing them with others who supported more radical methods. Purge from the opposite direction in July, 1950, followed the outbreak of the Korean War. The party's official newspaper, the *Akahata,* was forced to suspend publication at the same time that other measures were taken by the occupation to prevent Communist obstruction of the United Nations war effort. Since the peace treaty became effective in April, 1952, the party has again enjoyed the legal status of all other parties.

Composition of the House of Representatives, by parties, as of November, 1955, was as follows:

Liberal-Democratic Party	299
Socialist Party	154
Communist Party	2
Other parties	6
Independents	3
Vacancies	3
Total	467

READINGS

Quigley, Harold S., and John E. Turner. *The New Japan; Government and Politics.* Minneapolis, University of Minnesota Press, 1956.

Reischauer, Robert Karl. *Japan, Government—Politics.* New York, Thomas Nelson, 1939.

Scalapino, Robert A. *Democracy and the Party Movement in Prewar Japan; the Failure of the First Attempt.* Berkeley and Los Angeles, University of California Press, 1953.

Swearingen, Rodger, and Paul Langer. *Red Flag in Japan; International Communism in Action, 1919–1951.* Cambridge, Harvard University Press, 1952.

ECONOMIC LIFE

The economic development of Japan during the past hundred years has been one of the most remarkable feats in history. Two centuries of isolation and the financial and political ruin of the Tokugawa government gave the nation little but its wits, will, and manpower on which to build a strong, modern, industrialized state, but build one it did, and with meteoric speed. The principal impetus to this advance was the Meiji leaders' fear of the military strength of the Western Powers, already generations more highly developed than Japan. Laissez-faire commercial policies of the Powers gave Japan advantages that no underdeveloped nation has enjoyed since the First World War, and she made the most of them. She was a world power by 1919 and in the next two decades tried to acquire a still greater colonial empire, largely out of fear that she would be dependent on other nations for markets and raw materials. Japan's attempt to build a self-sufficient economy ultimately failed. The devastating war it engendered left her with many problems, but none has been so lastingly vexing as the inadequacy of her postwar economic circumstances. With a land area approximately the same as it was one hundred years ago she must support a population that is three times as large and growing at the rate of 1,300,000 a year. She must trade with other nations in ever increasing amounts merely to maintain her present standard of living, for her own meager natural resources are either stationary or declining; betterment of living conditions requires still greater trade expansion. The problem is further complicated by Japan's dependence to a greater extent than at any time within the last twenty years on international economic and political circumstances outside her control.

NATURAL RESOURCES AND EXTRACTIVE INDUSTRIES

The climate of Japan is favorable to agriculture and varies considerably with the 1,200-mile extension of the islands from north to south; however, periodic typhoons, tidal waves, floods, and earthquakes cause damage to both agriculture and industry.

Land Utilization (1952)

	Thousand Acres	Percent
Total area	90,527	100.0
Cultivated lands	13,343	14.8
Meadows and pastures	5,434	6.0
Forests	55,696	61.6
Other	16,054	17.6

It has been estimated that due to the mountainous character of the country, no more than 2 percent of the land remains that can profitably be brought under cultivation; however, the climate in the southern part of the country permits the growth of two crops a year; hence by double cropping the actual area is increased by about one third. The Japanese soil is not of high fertility, but the efficient Japanese farmer, through intensive cultivation and heavy use of natural and chemical fertilizers, has developed a high ratio of productivity. The terracing of upland fields, the use of dikes to reclaim marshland, and elaborate irrigation projects have all added to the cultivable land. The cultivated area was probably increased about 25 percent during the Meiji and Taishô periods, and perhaps another million acres (about 8 percent) have been either brought back under or added to cultivation since 1945.

Rice yields increased about one third from 1890 to 1940 and are two to three times as great per unit area as those of continental Asia. During the same period wheat, tea, and barley about doubled; crop yields as a whole increased about 65 percent. Rice is the principal food staple of Japan because it has the highest caloric value of the cereals. The year 1955 was a very good agricultural year, with a record rice crop of 666 million bushels; figures for other crops were: wheat, 54,890,000 bushels; barley, 98,980,000 bushels; soybeans, 19,000,000 bushels; oats, 10,680,000 bushels; corn, 3,430,000 bushels; and white potatoes, 2,884,000 metric tons. Sweet potatoes, of which about 6,000,000 metric tons per year are normally produced, were estimated at 6 percent greater than average. Vegetables and fruits are also grown in considerable quantities.

Sericulture is an important source of farm income. The 1955 spring crop of cocoons totaled 120 million pounds, an increase of 8.6 percent over 1954, and the fall crop has been estimated at 84 million pounds, the largest in the history of Japan. Tea, the other principal non-food crop, is down two fifths from the prewar high of 125 million pounds a year. Some tobacco is grown, and all of it is sold under government monopoly. Hemp, cotton, flax, jute, and ramie are also produced, but the output is far short of domestic needs.

Animal husbandry has received little attention in Japan because of the shortage of pasture land, but horses and cattle have always been much prized as draft animals. The government has attempted to encourage the increase of livestock, but is making slow progress. Livestock were estimated at the beginning of 1955 to include (in thousands of heads): cattle, 2,896; horses, 1,022; sheep, 733; goats, 532; pigs, 833; and poultry, 41,805. The dairy industry is very small. Animal products constitute only about 2 percent of the Japanese diet.

The average size of Japanese farms is 2.5 acres except in Hokkaido, where it is about 12 acres. Occupation land reformers found that only 33 percent of farmers owned all of the land they farmed, the remainder of the land being more or less controlled by landlords. To improve the farmers' lot, a reform was instituted by which the government bought up all land owned by absentee landlords and all but 2.5 acres per farm of tenant-farmed land owned by resident landlords (10 acres in Hokkaido). The government paid for the land in annuity bonds and resold it to tenant farmers, to be paid for in installments extending over a maximum period of 30 years. In all, some 4,500,000 acres changed hands under the program. Another reform forbade payment of rents in produce, limiting them to cash not to exceed 25 percent of the value of the rice crop plus 15 percent of the value of other crops.

The government has encouraged farm cooperatives since the beginning of this century, but their activities have expanded greatly since the war. They now handle a large part of all farm business, including purchases, sales of farm products, financial deposits, and loans.

In the past century agricultural production has probably increased by 200 percent, but the population has grown at about the same rate. From 1872 until the latter part of the Second World War the agricultural labor force remained stable at about 14,000,000, but a retreat from the devastation of the cities increased it to about 17,000,000.

Despite government efforts to improve their condition, farmers until after the Second World War were always the poorest and most oppressed part of the population. The hardships they suffered were an element in the discontent that led in the 1930's to rightist unrest at home and military adventures abroad. Today, farmers are comparatively prosperous. Food is relatively scarce, and the farmer has a permanent seller's market. The average size of Japanese farms is probably much too small for maximum efficiency, and the amount of labor expended has long since reached the point of diminishing returns. The only solution to this problem is the absorption of a portion of the agricultural labor force by industry. The government tries to encourage efficient farming by intensive scientific and technical research at its agricultural research stations, but no sudden or marked increase in productivity is likely.

To keep the average diet at about 2,200 calories per day, Japan since 1920 has been importing about 20 percent of her food supply. It is small wonder that, with a cultivable area smaller than West Virginia and a population of about 90,-000,000, she is deeply concerned with the increasing pressure on indigenous food resources. However, it might be pointed out

by way of comparison that England must import more than
three quarters of the wheat she consumes and 40 percent of her
meat, and that Japan is not so densely populated as either
Belgium or the Netherlands.

Japan's 55,000,000 acres of forests are one of her greatest natural resources and her principal source of building material,
household fuel, pulp, and paper. Reserves of standing timber
are estimated to exceed 700 billion board feet, but only 300
billion board feet stand in already developed forest lands.
For many years the forests were carefully maintained, and
cutting was limited to the estimated annual growth; however,
since the war, cutting has been excessive, about 10 billion
board feet a year, to replace war damage. There is no indica-
tion of any lessening of the demand. Erosion and floods are
added incentives to a vigorous government reforestation program. Domestic supplies of wood pulp have for years been
inadequate for paper and rayon production, the deficiencies
being supplied by imports.

Fish is an important supplement to the Japanese diet and
the principal source of protein food. The average Japanese eats
about sixty-five pounds of fish, but only five pounds of meat,
per year. (Average figures for the United States are twelve
pounds of fish and 140 pounds of meat.) The concentration of
population near the coast makes intensive fishing practical,
while the shortage of pasture land makes it necessary; for more
than forty years Japan has been the world's foremost fishing
country, and accounted for one fourth or more of its catches.
At the end of 1953 there were 660,000 people engaged in
operating 443,000 fishing boats totaling more than 1.2 million
tons; the total catch for that year was 4.2 million tons. While

the annual catch since 1951 has exceeded prewar figures (for example, 3.3 million tons in 1940), the increase in population has reduced the margin of marine products that Japan exports.

Mineral resources are very scarce. There are sufficient amounts of zinc, arsenic, bismuth, chromite, iron sulphide, limestone, cement, plaster of Paris, and sulphur to meet current industrial demand. Considerable quantities of iron, copper, manganese, and low-grade coal are available, but production costs of these minerals are high. Iron, manganese, lead, antimony, tin, mercury, gold, silver, cobalt, asbestos, petroleum, natural gas, and industrial salt are all in short supply. There is little or no platinum, nickel, tungsten, vanadium, molybdenum, aluminum ore, rock phosphate, potash, mica, fluorite, or magnesite.

The mining industry is currently producing about 15 percent above the 1934–36 average, but it is generally plagued with low quality ore deposits, high production costs, and labor troubles. Coal is, with hydroelectricity, the source of Japan's industrial power. At the present rate of consumption, about 43 million tons annually, there is an estimated two-hundred-year supply of coal, but it occurs mostly in narrow, broken seams and is of low caloric content, very little of it suitable for coke. Japan is a high-cost producer because of these factors, and the industry is somewhat depressed by competition from imported coal.

Japan produces 5 percent or less of her petroleum requirements. Since the war exploration has been intensive, but the increasing use of motor vehicles makes the domestic supply insignificant in relation to demand. Natural gas output reached

110 million cubic meters in 1953, thereby increasing to a certain extent the available supply of fuel and material for the petro-chemical industry, but the supply is very small.

Japan produces 20 percent or less of her iron ore requirements at present rates of consumption, and the domestic ore has to be beneficiated at high cost. Present production is about one million tons annually, and reserves are estimated at 80 million tons, more than half of it low-grade ore.

Copper production of approximately 100,000 tons a year is derived 65 percent from domestic ores, 31 percent from scrap, and 4 percent from imported ore. Japan was once a large exporter of copper, but domestic supplies are currently less than adequate for domestic consumption. Zinc is produced at the rate of about 75,000 tons a year, and reserves are estimated at 2.6 million tons. Lead is in short supply, with reserves of less than half a million tons. Japan depends entirely for aluminum production on bauxite imported from Malaya and Bintan Island. Total aluminum production capacity is about 280,000 tons, but only about 86,000 tons were produced in 1953. Japan could produce unlimited supplies of magnesium by the electrolytic sea-water process, but so far has not used this source. Manganese reserves are only 1.7 million tons, while the current annual consumption is about 200,000 tons, half of it from imported ores. Gold and silver production are nearly adequate to domestic industrial needs. Only 15 percent of tin requirements are produced from domestic sources.

Of the nonmetallic minerals, only pyrite, sulphur, and limestone are in ample supply. Output of sulphide ores in 1953 exceeded 2.3 million tons, of which 80 percent was consumed by the chemical fertilizer industry. Reserves of this ore are ample, being estimated at some 80 million tons. Limestone is in plentiful supply for the steel industry and cement manufacture. Salt is produced by the evaporation of sea water, the salt farms covering some 12,000 acres. Annual production is about 450,000 tons, but annual consumption is 2,000,000 tons, 45 percent for general use and 55 percent for industry. No phosphate rock or potash is produced domestically, so that these essential fertilizers must all be imported.

Japan is richly supplied with sources of hydroelectric power. The stored water capacity is estimated at 20 million kilowatts, of which 6.8 million kilowatts have already been developed.

INDUSTRY

Japanese industry has undergone many changes in structure since one hundred years ago. Then her economy was agricultural and some 70 to 80 percent of her economic activity consisted of farming and fishing. The following table showing the percentage distribution of the sources of national product gives some idea of the nature of the changes:

Percentage Distribution of National Product

	1878–82	1908–12	1933–37	1953
Total	100	100	100	100
Agriculture, fishing, forestry, and mining	38	39	21	26
Manufacturing and construction	13	23	36	28
Services	49	38	43	46

It is a generally accepted economic theory that during a period of industrial development the extractive industries will decline in relative importance, while manufacturing and construction rise. Such appears to have taken place in Japan. The slight rise in the extractive industries in 1953 would seem to reflect a more than proportional rise in prices of farm products following the war rather than any increase in their relative importance in the economy.

Japanese industry has shown a remarkable recovery and expansion since the end of the war, as will be seen from the index of industrial production for mining and manufacturing, which was 37.4 in 1947 (1934–36 taken to be 100) and 180.7 for 1955. The recovery of individual components may be judged from the following index numbers for 1955 on the same base: textiles, 85.9; metals, 218.7; machinery, 249.7; food and tobacco, 206.7; chemicals, 318.4; and ceramics, 174.8. The year 1956 shows further advances.

Since 1930 the character of the manufacturing industry has also changed rapidly. In 1930 the value of product was divided between light and heavy industry in the ratio of 62 to 38, but by 1942 this ratio had shifted to 27 to 73. At the same time the value of total product had increased from an index of 100 in 1930 to 273 in 1942; however, this increase was unevenly divided, for light industry increased from 100 to 121 while heavy industry's increase was from 100 to 519. It will be seen from these figures that light industry, primarily textiles, remained relatively stationary during the period, while the metal and engineering industries made rapid progress. The stimulus for this change was largely derived from the demands of the military in connection with the developing war in the Far East; nevertheless, it wrought a permanent change in the manufacturing structure. Although similar figures for the postwar period are not available, the continuation of this trend is apparent from the index figures in the preceding paragraph.

The textile industry has been the single most important factor in Japan's industrial development, representing in 1954 some 35 percent in value of her total industrial output. Textiles accounted for about 70 percent of Japan's total exports up to 1930, but had fallen to 60 percent by 1937, and are now about 40 percent. She now operates 8,000,000 spindles compared with the prewar peak in 1938 of 12,776,000. Japan is the world's greatest cotton cloth exporter, but world trade in cotton cloth has declined more than 43 percent since the thirties while world production of this fabric has increased by 37 percent. These facts account for the slow recovery of the textile industry in Japan, which is now operating at about 85 percent of the prewar average. Historically the silk industry was Japan's greatest asset, for until 1930 it paid for more than one third of all Japanese imports; however, the invention of the synthetic fibers together with depression and war has greatly diminished the silk trade. Raw silk production is about one third of the prewar peak, but the Japanese believe that further rationalization of the silk industry can cut costs to the point where exports can be doubled. In chemical fibers too Japan was the world's greatest exporter before the war, having turned to them with the decline of silk manufacture. The industry has almost fully recovered its prewar position, both in volume of production and exports. Output of woolen textiles exceeds the prewar levels and is a growing source of revenue in the export market.

Japan had recovered her prewar position in iron and steel production by 1953 with an output of 7,662,000 tons of steel, and she is continuing to expand her capacity. She ranks first among world shipbuilders, having passed Germany in 1955 and Great Britain in 1956. Metal and machinery manufacturing and chemicals have all more than doubled their prewar production figures. Precision instruments and optical goods are a growing source of revenue.

In spite of these advances, Japan is still ten years behind the other industrial nations in technology. Her costs of production are high because of obsolescence of equipment and techniques, despite large capital expenditures since the war to replace and renovate her plants. For this reason, it is difficult for her to compete in world markets for export trade. Poor in almost all of the raw materials needed, Japan's future industrial growth would appear to be best directed toward those products to which the greatest value is added in manufacture, such as heavy machinery, electrical equipment, precision instruments, and optics. The outlook for continued large textile exports is not bright, as many of the backward nations of the world that were formerly Japan's principal customers are rapidly developing their own textile industries. It is interesting to note that it is plant and equipment items which the countries of Southeast Asia have demanded of Japan as war reparations, and it is among these products and in this part of the world that much of Japan's future export market potential would seem to reside.

Since the Tokugawa regime forbade foreign intercourse, Japan
entered the modern era with no overseas shipping and only the
most rudimentary facilities for internal transportation. The
first Japanese railroad was constructed in 1870. From 1906 to
1909 the government purchased the main trunk lines that it
did not already own, and all government lines are now
operated by the Japan National Railway Corporation (NRC).
In addition there are about 140 private railway companies,
which operate feeder lines to the NRC. Total railway mileage
is 18,600, of which the NRC operates 14,000. The network of
lines is adequate for Japan's needs and compares favorably
with European coverage. Revenue from passengers exceeds
that from freight because coastal shipping rates on bulk traffic
are cheaper than railroad tariffs. Damage to rolling stock was
great during the war, but has been largely repaired. The NRC
owns 5,100 steam locomotives, 400 electric locomotives, 2,700
electric cars, 12,000 passenger cars, and 110,000 freight cars.
About 575,000 people are employed by all the railways.

Motor transportation is of growing importance in Japan;
bus and truck routes are operated by the NRC, local governments, and many private companies. However, any considerable further development depends upon the construction
of a much larger and better highway system. There are about
87,000 miles of national and prefectural roads capable of han-
dling motor vehicles, but only 12,400 miles are paved, and
hardly any are suited to modern traffic. The government has

instituted a five-year program of maintenance and repair, but progress is slow because of high costs.

A merchant marine was early considered of vital importance to an island country, both for defense and for commerce. The first Japanese steamship was built in 1866, and in 1884 and 1885, respectively, the Osaka Shôsen Kaisha and Nippon Yûsen Kaisha were formed. Shipping has always been heavily subsidized by the government, but has been a substantial source of revenue in the balance of payments. Before the war, Japan's merchant marine amounted to 6,094,000 gross tons and carried 63 percent of her imports and 73 percent of her exports. Revenues averaged 127 million yen annually from 1927 to 1936. The merchant marine ended the war with only 1,300,000 gross tons, mostly wartime and superannuated vessels. Revival of the shipping industry has been slow. At the end of 1954 there were only 3,292,000 gross tons in operation, little more than at the end of the First World War. In 1954 about 50 percent of Japan's foreign trade was shipped in her own vessels. Coastwise shipping has largely recovered since the war, and the capacity seems to be equal to the business available.

Postwar civil aviation in Japan dates from the establishment of the Japan Air Lines in 1951. This company, in addition to its domestic flights, operates flights to San Francisco, Okinawa, Hong Kong, and Bangkok. There are also about twenty smaller airlines in Japan.

PUBLIC UTILITIES AND COMMUNICATIONS

Japan is mountainous and has abundant rainfall, and hence has ample sources of hydroelectric power. There are 35 electric power enterprises in the country, but most electric generation and distribution is controlled by nine regional companies. A vast network of transmission lines covers the entire country, and only 2 percent of houses are without electricity, the lowest percentage in the world. Electricity is also the principal source of industrial power. Total generating capacity was 13,305,000 kilowatts in 1954; the installed ratio of water to thermal generation was about two to one; however, the ratio of power produced was three of water power to one of thermal, as the thermal capacity in many areas is used principally as insurance against dry seasons. Only one seventh of the power produced is consumed by households, which however pay 40 percent of the costs, because rates for lighting purposes are in a ratio to those for industry of about five to two. In 1952 Japan began a five-year program to expand electric power by 5,500,000 kilowatts, of which 3,600,000 kilowatts had been installed by the end of 1955. A loan by the World Bank of $55 million and extensive government loans to the industry have financed much of the program. Increase in power facilities will have to be almost continuous to provide for necessary industrial development. There is much interest in Japan in the future development of atomic power.

There are 80 gas enterprises which supply 150 cities and towns with fuel. Most of the gas is produced by the carbonization of coal, since the supply of natural gas is limited. Japan has been backward in the development of public water works, and only about 27 percent of the population uses public water systems.

Telephone and telegraph services were operated by the government from 1869 to 1952, when they were transferred to the Nippon Telegraph and Telephone Public Corporation. Japan's communications services are far behind those of the United States and most European countries. War damage has been largely repaired, but current demand is greater by 50 percent or more than before the war. Facilities are still very poor, and service is slow, but rapid improvement is being made. There are now about 2,500,000 telephones in Japan, and there is a program to increase the number by 700,000 as rapidly as possible. International telecommunications are in the hands of the International Telegraph and Telephone Corporation, which now handles 50 percent more telegrams than before the war and 36 times as many telephone calls as in the prewar peak year, 1937. Radio and television broadcasting is conducted by the Japan Broadcasting Corporation, which was formerly a government monopoly, and by several new commercial broadcasting stations.

LABOR

The current Japanese labor force of approximately 40 million is about one-third female. In 1950, 48 percent of the labor force were employed in agriculture, forestry, and fishing; 21 percent in mining, manufacturing, and construction; 30 percent in trade, banking, transportation, communications, government, and other services; and about 700,000 (less than 1 percent) were stated to be unemployed. The last figure is thought to be too low, however, for the addition to agriculture of 3 million since the war probably includes many who are actually unemployed. Furthermore, Japanese unemployment figures ignore those partially employed.

The index of productivity of labor rose to 133.7 in 1954 (1934–36 taken to be 100), but Japanese labor is thought to be only about one-third as productive as that of Europe, and even further behind the productivity of labor in the United States, though comparisons of this sort are difficult to make and are often of doubtful value.

The Japanese labor movement was slow to develop. The government, where it did not actually suppress it, did nothing to encourage it. Furthermore, domestic industry was the pattern that tradition imposed, and the factory system was consequently late in emerging. By 1900 there were still less than half a million factory workers; even today many firms employ no more than five persons. In the textile industry, moreover, up to 80 percent of the employees have been female, many of them young girls.

Safety regulations in industry, limitation of hours of work, and the protection and limitation of child labor all developed late against the strong resistance of factory and mine owners. However, the Mining Act of 1905 did provide some safeguards for workers, and the First Factory Act of 1916 provided for limitation of working hours, minimum age for children in industry, and protection of women.

The rise in the cost of living during the First World War was accompanied by renewed labor agitation, and by 1918 a Federated Association of Workers had been created. In 1929 it comprised 630 associations with 330,987 members. Labor came under increasingly strict government regulations in the thirties, and with the outbreak of war in 1941, unions were suppressed altogether.

The enactment of the Trade Union Law in 1946 provided

the necessary stimulus for resurgence of labor unions, which grew from a membership of 380,000 at the end of 1945 to 6,700,000 in June, 1948. In February, 1947, a general strike was averted only by the direct intervention of General MacArthur, and in 1948 the necessity of stopping the inflation brought restrictions on wage increases and resultant dampening of the labor movement. In spite of this, labor has remained strong, and in June, 1954, there were more than 31,000 unions with almost 6,000,000 members. Public service workers' unions (transportation and communications), which enroll 80 percent of the personnel in the field, are the best organized, followed by miners (78 percent), government workers (43 percent), service enterprise workers (41 percent), manufacturing workers (39 percent), construction workers (29 percent), and fishermen and marine workers (22 percent).

Communists gained control of some unions after the war, but their influence had been eliminated for the most part by 1948, and there has been a much stronger feeling against them in most unions since the outbreak of the Korean War.

Wages increased rapidly with the postwar inflation, but were not able to keep pace with prices, and real wages still seem to be somewhat below the 1934–36 average. The labor force is growing at the rate of seven to eight hundred thousand a year. To ensure a livelihood to this group is Japan's most pressing problem, the only solution to which seems to be a constantly expanding industry. The continuous rise in unemployment figures indicates that industry is not keeping pace with the rise in the labor force, and that a growing source of future trouble may be developing. This is all the more alarming because it exists simultaneously with a world-wide industrial boom. What will happen if there is a serious industrial recession in Japan and what solutions will be found to meet such a situation are among the most serious problems facing the country.

The economic revolution of early Meiji necessitated a completely new system of financial institutions. In the 1870's, the nation faced serious financial problems. Heavy military expenditures, the assumption of clan debts, and pensions to the old aristocracy in return for the renunciation of their feudal dues caused government expenses to exceed revenues by far, and the deficit was met with issues of paper money.

In 1877 a national banking system was established patterned on that of the United States, and the new national banks were permitted to issue their own notes. Former samurai had previously received government bonds in commutation of their pensions, and though as a class they had little business experience, their new capital holdings enabled them to undertake organization of most of the national banks. Under Count Matsukata, Finance Minister from 1881, the financial disorders resulting from a too loosely organized system were brought under control. The Bank of Japan, established in 1882 as the central bank of the country and modeled after the Bank of Belgium, gradually retired the depreciated paper currency by the issue of notes. The banking system was reorganized, the government debt refunded, and the tax system revised. The gold indemnity that Japan received from China as reparations for the Sino-Japanese War of 1894–95 enabled Japan to abandon the silver standard and to establish the gold standard.

The Bank of Japan had sole charge of note issues and was the fiscal agent for the government. A number of quasi-official banks for special purposes included: the Yokohama Specie Bank (1880), the chief foreign exchange bank; the Hypothec Bank (1896), central organ for the forty-seven Agricultural and Industrial Banks which were set up to make low-interest loans on immovable property; and the Industrial Bank of Japan, which financed large-scale industry and some colonial development. In the colonies were the Bank of Formosa, the Oriental Development Company, and the Bank of Korea. Finally, the Deposit Bureau of the Ministry of Finance served as a postal savings organization which channeled small savings into government bonds and other semi-official holdings. By 1933 these institutions held one third of all the paid-up capital and reserves of all Japanese banks. While privately capitalized, they were under close governmental supervision and were active instruments of national policy.

Commercial banking expanded rapidly in Japan, and by 1920 there were more than two thousand banks in the country; however, bank failures and mergers in the financial crisis of 1927 reduced this number to about one thousand. During the Manchurian Incident, banks were grouped by prefectures for stricter government control. In 1935, there were only 655, and by 1944 these were further reduced to 61. These were of three classes: the special banks; zaibatsu-controlled banks, whose influence dominated commerce and industry; and the ordinary commercial banks.

All this has changed since the war. The law under which special banks operated has been repealed, and the zaibatsu banks have become comparatively weak because of the breakup of the combines. The Japanese banking system now bears many similarities to English and European systems. There are 86 commercial banks in Japan. Two of these, with 15 branches, issue finance bonds; thirteen more, with 1,791 branches, are reorganized zaibatsu banks and other major banks; there are sixty-five local banks with 3,579 branches and 57 subbranches; finally, six, with 98 branches, are trust banks.

Japan has twenty life insurance companies and twenty property insurance companies. One special private institution is the Central Cooperative Bank for Agriculture and Forestry, which is the coordinating center for farmers' cooperatives. Since the war, the government has established a number of financial institutions to aid in economic rehabilitation. Among these are the Trust Fund Bureau, the People's Finance Corporation, the Japan Development Bank, and the Japan Export and Import Bank.

Before the war, credit was comparatively easy to obtain, but at very high interest rates, and there was mild inflation throughout most of the period. The end of the war brought on serious inflation due to central bank loans to the commercial banks to aid in reconstruction and due to excessive government deficits that reconstruction entailed. The yen-dollar exchange rate was 4 to 1 in 1939, but depreciated after the war to 360 to 1, where it was finally stabilized in 1949 under stringent occupation controls.

The present currency system in Japan is a "maximum issue limitation" system. The currency consists of Bank of Japan notes and auxiliary coin. The limit of issue of bank notes is determined by the Minister of Finance, and is currently 510 billion yen. The Bank of Japan can issue notes in excess of this amount, but if the excess issue extends over 15 days, a tax of 3 percent is levied on the excess amount issued. Against the amount of issued currency there must be held an equivalent amount of commercial drafts, loans, state bonds, foreign exchange, gold, silver, etc. The total currency issue as of December 31, 1955, was 673.8 billion yen.

A striking feature of the prewar economy was the concentration of private capital in a few large combines, the zaibatsu firms, all of them under the hereditary control of what was virtually a finance caste. They rose to their dominant position through governmental favor, business acumen, and a system of inheritance which permitted the continued concentration of financial control through primogeniture or the formation of family holding companies. The fifteen largest combines, including the Mitsui, Mitsubishi, Sumitomo, and Yasuda, are estimated to have accounted for three quarters of Japan's business transactions. Companies in zaibatsu hands were not limited to heavy and light manufacturing concerns, but included shipping, wholesale, retail, and warehouse firms; banks; insurance companies; trust companies; and real estate concerns.

The occupation undertook after the war to break up the extreme concentration of economic power in the hands of this financial clique. To this end, the large holding companies were ordered dissolved, members of the zaibatsu families were barred from holding office in any of their former companies or in the government, private monopolies were forbidden, and a graduated capital tax took 90 percent of the wealth of individuals with more than 15 million yen. Since the peace treaty, however, many of the restrictions against zaibatsu families and concerns have been removed, and the anti-monopoly laws have been eased to permit the formation of cartels. Although it is unlikely that the principal zaibatsu families will ever regain their former power, the groups do seem to be forming again as communities of interest, and the old familiar names are reappearing. To the credit of the zaibatsu, it must be said that some of the best business and technical brains of Japan are in this group and that much of the past development of the country has been due to their efforts.

PUBLIC FINANCE

The government of Japan has always played an active part in fostering the economic development of the country, but since the turn of the century its role has been largely indirect except for the operation of arsenals, the steel industry, railroads, public utilities, and government monopolies of tobacco, alcohol, salt, and camphor. Since the war it has again been actively participating in the financial rehabilitation of the economy. This participation has resulted in large deficits for most of the postwar years. However, a tight money policy was instituted in 1953 to stop renewed threats of inflation, and the general financial picture is now much brighter, for Japan has accumulated large reserves of foreign exchange. Another contributing cause of the improvement is the realization of earlier efforts to rationalize industry and recapture or develop export markets.

The internal public debt was 919.7 billion yen at the end of 1955, having increased by 100 billion yen since the end of 1954. All prewar external bonded debt was assumed by the government, and payments are now being made in full. The prewar external government bonded debt was 62,651,000 dollars, 54,907,000 pounds, and 383,221,000 francs at the end of 1955. The postwar debt situation is confused, for it includes unsettled reparations claims, loans from the Export-Import Bank of Washington and the International Bank for Reconstruction and Development, and the settlement of other U.S. accounts.

In reparations, Burma is to receive $250,000,000 in goods, services, and loans over a ten-year period; and Thailand is to receive $41,666,666 in cash, goods, and services over a period of years. Japan has concluded a settlement with the Philippines which grants that country $550,000,000 in capital goods and services over a twenty-year period and a separate agreement to grant $250,000,000 for capital goods in long-term credits from private industrial resources in Japan. Indonesian claims are as yet unsettled. The reparations agreements have been made in the only way in which they could ever actually be paid, for the recipients have indicated a willingness to accept payment largely in goods and services. The only outstanding problem with Indonesia is agreement on the amount to be paid. It behooves Japan to arrive at an early settlement of this matter, for it hinders the full development of trade with an area which may in future years be among her principal sources of raw materials as well as a market for her exports.

DOMESTIC AND FOREIGN TRADE

Though Japanese talk much of the importance of foreign trade to their country's economic welfare, 70 to 80 percent of Japan's national income is actually derived from domestic trade. Furthermore, national income has already comfortably passed the prewar level (in terms of 1934–36 prices), both in total figures and per capita: in 1935 the national income was 14,300 million yen; in 1954 it was 19,500 million yen; the 1935 per capita income was 209 yen; in 1954 it was 223 yen.

In the decade before the war, exports and imports averaged about 20 percent and 21 percent, respectively, of national income. In 1953 exports were 8 percent and imports 15 percent of national income, and the situation has improved markedly in 1954 and 1955, exports having increased by about 30 percent in each of those years and imports having decreased somewhat. Except during the First World War, Japanese imports have always exceeded exports, and the balance has been met at various periods by foreign borrowings, by drawing down foreign balances, and by shipping and insurance earnings. Japan's present weakness in foreign trade can be attributed to the following factors: restrictive bilateral trade agreements and currency clearing arrangements; structural changes in the character of world trade, notably the dislocations caused by rehabilitation after the war, the blockade between the communist areas and the rest of the world, and the industrialization of backward areas; the poorer competitive position of Japanese products due to high production costs and to an apparently unrealistic foreign exchange rate; and difficult problems in foreign relations, particularly in Southeast Asia.

As Japan has proceeded with her industrial development, the major items of export and import have undergone radical changes. In the early years she exported raw materials and textiles, while her imports were largely manufactured products, such as machinery, ships, industrial equipment, and (perhaps most important of all) an invisible item, the technology of the West. Until 1930 textiles comprised 70 percent or more of her exports, and the great bulk of the remainder were the products of light industry. Japan's great advantages were the generally unrestricted conditions of world trade and a profitable silk trade involving as it did no importation of raw materials. The breakdown of multilateral trade during the depression of the 1930's and the substitution of rayon and nylon for silk dealt heavy blows to Japan's foreign trade; however, she devalued the yen, accepted adverse terms of trade, turned to rayon production, developed her heavy industry, and thus created an industrial boom in the decade before the war.

In 1955 Japan's exports were divided approximately as follows: textiles, 37 percent; metals and metal products, 20 percent; machinery, 12 percent; foodstuffs, 7 percent; chemicals, 5 percent; nonmetallic products, 4 percent; and ceramics, 3 percent. Imports were as follows: foodstuffs, 26 percent; textile raw materials, 25 percent; fuels, 11 percent; metallic minerals, 7 percent; nonmetallic minerals, 4 percent; other raw materials, 14 percent; and machinery, 6 percent. In short, Japan is an exporter of light and heavy manufactured products (increasingly concentrating on products of heavy industry) and an importer of the food and raw materials consumed by her people and her industries.

As Japan's demand and supply patterns have changed, there have also been marked changes in the geographic distribution of her foreign trade. The following table shows these changes on a percentage basis for selected years:

Overseas Trade of Japan Proper
Percentage Distribution by Regions
1893, 1913, 1936, and 1955

	EXPORTS				IMPORTS			
	1893	1913	1936	1955	1893	1913	1936	1955
All countries	100	100	100	100	100	100	100	100
Asia	31	50	63	42	43	52	53	37
Japanese colonies —Korea and Formosa	...	12	25	5	...	8	24	4
China (including Manchuria and Hong Kong)	26	30	20	6	29	12	11	4
India (and Pakistan in 1954)	2	4	7	6	11	22	10	5
Southeast Asia	...	3	8	18	1	10	7	17
United States	32	26	17	22	7	15	23	31
Europe	32	21	9	10	47	28	9	7
United Kingdom	6	5	4	3	29	16	2	2
British Dominions	3	2	4	7	...	2	8	13
Other	2	1	7	19	3	3	6	12

It will be noted that exports to the United States, Europe, and China all decreased through most of the period. Imports from the United States have steadily increased, while those from Europe have declined. It is also apparent that Southeast Asia has replaced China and the former colonies of Formosa and Korea as the major Asiatic market. The loss of the China market and the restrictive policies currently in force on trade with the communist bloc are the occasion of much regret in Japan. However, it seems unlikely that trade with Communist China would amount to very much, even if the restrictions were removed, for that country is bent on her own industrialization and would scarcely be willing to part with any large amounts of the raw materials formerly bought by Japan or to furnish a large market for Japanese consumer goods. While China might for a time be a market for Japanese heavy manufactures in her efforts to industrialize, such trade might be negotiated on terms which the Japanese would ultimately find unprofitable. Increased postwar trade with unspecified areas (last line of table) reflects continuation of the world-wide dispersal of sources and markets, particularly the growth of trade with South America and Africa.

The trade balance in Japan has traditionally shown a large deficit, which before the war was compensated for largely by shipping and insurance receipts, but which in the postwar period has been met by U.S. aid, purchase of war materials in Japan for the Korean War, advances for the maintenance of U.S. forces in Japan, and the local spending of American troops. United States aid grants to Japan have totaled more than two billion dollars since the war, and receipts from U.S. forces have totaled $600–800 million annually in recent years. As income from these sources is outside the control of the Japanese, it is not difficult to see why they feel insecure about their balance-of-payments position. However, Japan had been able to accumulate by the end of 1955 more than $1.4 billion of foreign exchange. For the year 1955 Japan showed a favorable trade balance of $100 million and in the international balance of payments had a $500 million surplus. This favorable position is due in part to the world boom in trade, good Japanese harvests in 1955, and some drawing down of inventories of raw materials, but there are strong reasons to hope that Japan is recovering her equilibrium in foreign trade.

Except from 1899 to 1913 when the government borrowed heavily abroad to defray deficits arising from military expenditures and again in the 1920's, when some foreign loans were floated for electric power development, foreign capital borrowing has not played any considerable part in the development of Japan. From the First World War to the end of the Pacific War, Japan was a creditor nation on capital account; however, since 1945 she has again borrowed heavily abroad. While her leaders now say that they would like to attract foreign capital investment in Japanese industry, and while her need for large amounts of capital is unquestionable, equity capital is not wanted. Japan has traditionally feared foreign interference in her domestic affairs, and the sincerity of her desire for any considerable foreign investment in her industry seems somewhat dubious.

The developing interdependence of the countries of the non-communist world on trade, capital investments, and interchange of technical knowledge should not be a cause for fear for any nation. Because Japan is more dependent on foreign trade than some of the other members of this group, she would seem to have a greater stake in promoting a return to multilateral trade relations and free convertibility of currencies than most of the others. As the most advanced industrial nation in

Asia, she can also contribute greatly to the industrial development of her neighbors. It is in these directions that Japan may find solutions to many of her current economic problems.

READINGS

Ackerman, Edward A. *Japan's Natural Resources and Their Relation to Japan's Economic Future.* Chicago, University of Chicago Press, 1953.

Allen, George C. *A Short Economic History of Modern Japan.* London, George Allen & Unwin, 1946.

Cohen, Jerome B. *Japan's Economy in War and Reconstruction.* Minneapolis, University of Minnesota Press, 1949.

The Japan Annual 1955. Tokyo, 1956.

Lockwood, William W. *The Economic Development of Japan.* Princeton, Princeton University Press, 1954.

Moulton, Harold G., and Junichi Ko. *Japan, an Economic and Financial Appraisal.* Washington, Brookings Institution, 1931.

Schumpeter, Elizabeth B. (ed.). *The Industrialization of Japan and Manchukuo, 1930–1940.* New York, Macmillan, 1940.

PERIODICALS

Bank of Japan. *Economic Statistics of Japan,* annual. Tokyo, Bank of Japan, 1925—.

Bank of Japan. *Quarterly Review.* Tokyo, Bank of Japan, 1948—.

Journal of Finance and Commerce, monthly. Tokyo, Nippon Times, 1948—.

Mitsubishi Economic Research Bureau. *Monthly Circular. Analytical and Statistical Survey of Economic Conditions in Japan.* Tokyo, 1–210, 1924–41; 211—, 1947—.

The Oriental Economist, monthly. Tokyo, The Oriental Economist, 1934—.

SOCIAL AND
CULTURAL LIFE

The physical characteristics of the Japanese people most closely resemble those of the Mongoloid race of China and northeast Asia. Mongoloid features present in most Japanese include straight black hair, dark-brown eyes, the "slant-eyed" appearance of the fold in the eyelids at the inner canthus, low nasal bridge, yellowish-brown skin, and the Mongoloid spot found at the base of the spine of many new-born infants. However, certain common features differ from those of other Mongoloids. Strains of the Caucasoid Ainus may account for the relative hairiness of Japanese among Mongoloid peoples, although numbers of wavy-haired Japanese presumably derive from an admixture of southern Asiatic stock. In addition, Japanese are typically shorter than North Chinese and Mongolians, averaging (for men) five feet five inches.

Archaeology too indicates a north Asiatic origin for some of the ancestors of the modern Japanese. Cultural anthropologists find it significant, however, that certain culture traits—in mythology and domestic architecture, for example—resemble those of Malaysia and Polynesia and are quite dissimilar from those of China and Korea.

SOME ASPECTS OF THE NATIONAL CHARACTER

Time has blended the strains from which the Japanese race has descended into a homogeneous nation. There is a danger in speaking of the national traits of any people, but if one grants from the start that individual exceptions exist in plenty to every rule of Japanese behavior, certain meaningful generalizations remain. The Japanese display strong national pride and sensitivity; they are given both to undue chauvinism for national achievements and to painful embarrassment at what they conceive to be national shortcomings. More positively, they are genuinely concerned with the interests of their whole society, placing them before family interests or the advantage of provinces or classes.

Dishonesty is not characteristic of the Japanese. "Polite lies" have a place in the deportment of all nations; the Japanese resort to them in social situations where the expression of a flatly contradictory opinion would be considered intolerable rudeness. To Americans, whose social usages prescribe a greater degree of frankness and directness, such evasions sometimes inspire an unjustified distrust of Japanese sincerity. In fact, some national practices indicate personal honesty and scrupulousness to the letter of the law greater than in our own culture. A few public telephones still survive from the time when, in the absence of coined money, one made pay-station telephone calls on the honor system, depositing bills in boxes supplied beside the phone.

The Japanese dislike intensely the embarrassments of personal rebuff and confessions of failure and employ many devices to avoid causing or receiving loss of face. Among them is the extensive use of go-betweens in business and social relations.

Many observers have pointed out a dominant aesthetic sense in the Japanese temperament. Universal appreciation and preservation of the natural beauty of their homeland and a love of aesthetically pleasing pastimes (flower viewing, flower arranging, the tea ceremony, for instance) are striking instances of this. In addition, they maintain traditions of fine style in the manufacture of everyday utilitarian objects.

Most of the components of traditional Japanese higher culture have their origins in Korea or China. Early contacts with China brought Japan directly out of the stone age and gave her the rudiments of her art, industry, and government. Even indigenous institutions, such as the native religion and the Imperial House, were profoundly modified by contact with Chinese counterparts. Yet the insularity of the Japanese always prevented their civilization from becoming identical with that of the Continent. Modern Chinese and Japanese civilizations illustrate the possibility of wide divergence from a single cultural background.

The westernization of Japan has seemingly touched all phases of the national life. Rapid transportation and communications, machine industry, and the study of fascism, socialism, and democratic liberalism have had profound effects on national habits. The cultivation of Western dress, music, and amusements are more superficial aspects of the same process. Naturally, much remains that is characteristically oriental, and this will doubtless modify whatever Western traits become naturalized.

The Japanese have been characterized, usually contemptuously, as an "imitative" people. Certainly they have been successful in adapting to their own purposes traits from many different cultures. On the other hand, there are elements in every department of their civilization that have no exact equivalents in any other country: the classic drama and poetic forms in literature, a cuisine making distinctive use of sea foods, a native sect—that of Nichiren—within the Buddhist faith, even inventions and technological advances based on Western scientific knowledge. It would be more accurate to say that Japanese civilization, neither unique nor indigenous, has hitherto been part of the civilization of East Asia and that it is now perhaps responding to new challenges by becoming part of a new Pacific civilization. Japan has used whatever the other parts of those civilizations had to offer in the way of material and ideological advances, and in her turn has contributed inventions and ideas of her own to them. Some Japanese, it is true, are faddists. In the history of Japanese fashion, these have imitated everything from Chinese prose poems to left-bank novels and from Hindu musical instruments to pinball machines. Genuine assimilation of foreign culture, however, is another matter entirely. It has been a major aspect of the extraordinary vitality and adaptability of Japanese civilization.

SOCIAL CLASSES

It is common for foreigners to suppose that there are by and large two classes of Japanese society—rich and poor. There is in fact an important middle class in the small businesses and the professions. An economic gulf separates these from the vast farmer and laborer group, whose poverty makes them a genuine proletariat.

Until three generations ago the dominant Confucian ideology called for a static division of society into three classes. The highest of these was the samurai, who controlled the land, manned the learned professions, and administered the government; next came the peasantry, the main productive class, romantically adulated by their betters at the same time that they were kept in subservience to them; lowest were the townsmen, artisans and merchants. Society in the eighteenth and nineteenth centuries was actually more fluid than this. The growing wealth of certain members of the merchant class had already begun to give them prestige approaching that of the samurai. With the abolition of feudalism in the 1870's, samurai, to make a living, were forced into business, the professions, or the laboring class. A new ruling class took the place of the old feudal order and consisted of men of comparatively new wealth, with some of the more prosperous members of the old feudal and court nobility. Japanese society is still much less fluid than American, though new families have succeeded in making their way through to the aristocracy.

Another elite group in Japan is the official class. Sons of good families accept the inferior salaries of government positions for the sake of the prestige and security that membership in the bureaucracy traditionally entails. Even the policeman is looked up to by the public. Artists, scholars, and teachers too enjoy social prestige out of proportion to their economic position.

Feudal society included two pariah classes, the *eta* and the *hinin*. The former were a hereditary caste, performing several of the menial occupations that were taboo to orthodox Buddhists. Among these occupations were the slaughter of animals, the execution of criminals, and curiously, the manufacture and sale of footgear. The *hinin* were not a hereditary group but consisted of individuals who had lost caste by becoming beggars or criminals. Both classes were abolished as legal entities in the antifeudal decrees of early Meiji. Samurai, peasants, townsmen, and *eta* all alike became commoners. True social equality for the former *eta* has been much more difficult to achieve. Intermarriage with *eta* is still frowned upon by Japanese of other classes, and the ancient stigma still forces some of them into degrading occupations.

FAMILY ORGANIZATION

In Japan, as elsewhere, the family is the basic unit of society. Japanese law and custom, however, give the family greater authority over the lives of its members than in the West. American youths are legally free of parental authority at the age of twenty-one and in practice enjoy considerable independence of action years earlier. In Japan, on the other hand, men and women frequently depend for most of their adult lives on the judgments of their elders within the family. Japanese law defines as the fundamental kinship unit a household, domiciled together and normally headed by the eldest male within it. Household members include the wife of the family head, their eldest son and his family, and their other children, if unmarried. In custom, a Japanese woman belongs to her father's family until she is married and to that of her eldest son on the death of her husband. To ensure continuance of the male family line, couples without sons frequently resort to adoption.

If there are daughters, a son-in-law may be adopted to inherit the family property and carry on the family name. Elders may in effect abdicate the parental authority while they are alive. In this case, the eldest son becomes the family head and his parents nominally are subsidiary members of the household. Households are legal institutions as well as social entities. Rationing to households rather than individuals and the registry of vital statistics and census figures in terms of families are present-day survivals of an age when the legal functions of a family were still more important. In feudal times households even shared legal responsibility for the crimes of individual members.

The position of women in the Japanese family has been gradually liberalized over a period of decades. They have long had the right to own property and to initiate divorce actions. With suffrage in 1946, they came to enjoy legal rights with men, though there can be no doubt that custom continues to place greater restrictions on their freedom than in most Western countries.

A typical instance of the operation of family authority is the manner in which marriages are usually contracted. The parents choose a mate for a marriageable son or daughter from among the children of families of their acquaintance. They do not arrange the marriage directly with the parents of the prospective spouse but employ a trusted friend of both the families to act as middleman. Only when the marriage arrangements have been decided upon by both the families do the young people meet each other to approve the match. By recent law parents may not force their children into marriage against their wishes. Even so, by the force of custom, most marriages are still by parental arrangement. As the social system permits relatively little comradeship between young men and women, love-matches cannot be depended on to provide spouses for all. Even when young people become engaged by their own choice, the actual marriage details are frequently arranged in the traditional way.

Members of a household are not equal in their privileges and responsibilities. Instead each has his rank in relation to each of the others, status as a rule increasing with age. Boys take the responsibility for the care and household training of their younger brothers and expect obedience from them in return. Sisters within a family have a similar set of relationships. The head of the household is usually the highest wage earner. His opinions count for much in vital family decisions on the marriage of the children, choice of domicile, and the like. In addition, he enjoys highest prestige within the family, bathing first in the water the entire household shares and being served first at meals. His wife too has her areas of authority and responsibility. Since she spends most of the household's income, she naturally has the greatest freedom of decision as to how it is to be spent. Education of her children within the home is another of her provinces.

THE GREATER FAMILY

Kinship solidarity is by no means limited to the members of a single household. Members of one household, plus their aunts, uncles, and cousins to a fairly remote degree, comprise an extended family with important social functions. In a country with inadequate public facilities for the care of the aged, infirm, and indigent, security for these individuals is largely the responsibility of their relatives. If they have no immediate family on whom to rely, they must be taken care of by their more remote kin. (Farm communities and city neighborhoods frequently cooperate in similar fashion and assume group responsibility whenever individuals or families meet with ruinous calamities.) Related households cooperate closely in the management of property or businesses that they have inherited jointly.

Several instances survive from the days of hereditary trades, crafts, and occupations. In some highly specialized arts and crafts, a family apprenticeship system furnished the only practical means of training children from birth to carry on the family tradition. Actors in the traditional *kabuki* dramas, for example, are a guild of several interrelated families who maintain strict control over the casting of roles, the techniques of performances, and even the texts of the plays. Other such guilds are responsible for the continuance of traditions in painting, music, ceramics, and the like. In the inevitable cases in which families of artists or artisans fail to produce talented children to succeed them, they have recourse to the universally accepted custom of adoption.

The zaibatsu firms, which have supplied most of the capital, managed most of the trade and industry, and owned most of the wealth of modern Japan, are family corporations transmitting property in much the same way as in the family guilds. A few of these companies date from the early seventeenth century and have maintained strict inheritance of property and control until the very recent past. Venerable codes of house law prescribed relations of zaibatsu members within their families and with the outside world and, above all, guarded against the loss of control over the companies to outsiders. On the theory that Japan's concentration of wealth and industrial control was inimical to her development as a peaceful and democratic nation, the occupation forced zaibatsu companies to offer much of their stock for sale on the open exchange. The failure of this reform to effect any large-scale redistribution of economic control is evidence of the power of kinship solidarity in this important department of Japanese society.

EDUCATION

Before Meiji schools were of two kinds: aristocratic academies for the inculcation of Confucian virtue and the study of the Chinese classics, and Buddhist temple-schools for the young of other social classes. Vocational education was from father to son, and women acquired whatever talents were thought essential to their cultivation at the hands of their mothers. The Meiji government early realized the necessity of a trained citizenry if Japan was to be brought up to the standards of Western countries. It set up elementary and secondary schools throughout the country under the close scrutiny of the Ministry of Education. Government-run universities and technical colleges were opened to students from a wide variety of social classes by a combination of low tuition and high admission standards. Girls had easy access to primary education, but higher education facilities for them were meager. From the start the government schools emphasized the training necessary to produce loyal citizens. The defect in the system was that too close control by the central government allowed reactionary leaders to ensure the perpetuation of reaction. Japanese education was undemocratic simply because Japan was not a democracy. Occupation reforms of the school system aimed to make it democratic by (1) increasing school facilities and thus permitting more students to go to school longer and (2) divorcing primary and secondary education from central control.

The system, as modified under the occupation, provides nine years' free, compulsory schooling in primary and lower secondary schools. At this level schools are coeducational. Admission to the three-year upper secondary course is by competitive examination. Tuition is charged and schools may or may not be coeducational. Vocational education starts on the upper secondary level and continues in specialized colleges or the technical departments of universities. Colleges and universities now have four-year courses, entered after twelve years of primary and secondary schooling, instead of the old three-year course, which one entered after fourteen years in the lower schools. Graduate schools in some colleges and universities are a recent innovation. There are more than two hundred colleges and universities of all kinds, public and private, and these had a total enrollment in 1954 of nearly 500,000.

The elementary curriculum regularly includes Japanese reading and writing, arithmetic, social studies, science, music, drawing, handicrafts, and physical education. The teaching of reading and writing predominates, for Japanese writing is an even greater academic time-consumer than English spelling. A postwar reform abolished the teaching of military training and of *shûshin,* or "ethics," the latter because it included the inculcation of militaristic and chauvinistic ideals inconsistent with the occupation's program of democratization. Textbooks in all courses were revised to rid them of supernationalistic flavor. Standards of university scholarship are high, in accordance with the best Western traditions, German, English, and American. The introduction of coeducation in the national universities after the war offers women for the first time what the Japanese consider to be their highest quality of advanced instruction.

OCCUPATIONS

The proportion of employed Japanese in various types of occupations in 1950, as compared with 1940, is as follows:

	PERCENTAGE EMPLOYED	
	1950	*1940*
Agriculture and fishing	48.5	44.1
Mining	1.5	1.8
Construction	4.0	3.0
Manufacturing	15.8	21.2
Commerce and finance	11.8	13.6
Transportation and communications	5.0	4.7
Professions	9.0	9.0
Government service	4.1	1.9
Unclassified	0.3	0.7

RECREATIONS

Japanese folk toys attest to the ingenuity of the Japanese in using simple ideas and economical materials. Some are objects of true folk art, associated with local craft traditions. Native games, too, utilize simple basic ideas, though the two most famous of them, *shōgi*, or "Japanese chess," and *go*, are games of skill demanding intelligence and much practice for their mastery.

Traditional recreations for the masses center in the holidays and festival seasons. Some of these are of purely political or national significance and include the birthday of the present Emperor (April 29), Constitution Day (commemorating the enforcement of the new Constitution on May 3, 1947), and Culture Day (November 3, dedicated to the promotion of culture as a concern of a peace-loving people). Celebrations at the vernal and autumnal equinoxes are religious festivals. The former is traditionally the time for nation-wide veneration of ancestors. Labor Thanksgiving Day (November 23) perpetuates the old Shinto ceremonies of dedication of crops. Children's Day (May 5) is a national holiday on the date of the old Boys' Festival, featuring kite-flying competition. Girls' Day (March 3) is a time for displaying dolls. Most important of the holiday seasons is the New Year, which lasts most of the month of January. Religious and secular observances associated with this season include formal calls on business and social acquaintances, family visits to neighborhood shrines, games of battledore and shuttlecock, and the consumption of much *mochi,* the glutinous rice-cakes reserved for this time of year.

Flower arranging, the tea ceremony, gardening (on a very small scale), the chanting of *yōkyoku* (texts of the classical *nō* dramas), photography, and calligraphy are among the minor arts cultivated by many Japanese as hobbies.

Traditional sports were encouraged before the war as aids to the cultivation of military spirit and self-control. Most famous of these were *jūdō* and *kendō,* or fencing. *Sumō,* the major native spectator sport, is a highly stylized form of wrestling practiced by giants purposely trained and overfed from childhood by the family guilds into which they are adopted. Western sports are universally popular. Baseball, both of the sand-lot variety played by practically all boys and as a spectator sport by college teams, is the national game. The physical characteristics of the Japanese especially suit them to sports of speed and agility such as tennis and swimming.

WAY OF LIFE AND LIVING STANDARD

Evaluation of Japan's living standard depends on the norm one wishes to apply. Though restricted in comparison to some European and American countries, Japan comes closer to providing the essentials for comfort than most other countries of the Far East. Ignoring for a moment the very real deficiency in diet available to the average Japanese, it can be said that the relatively simple and economical way of life allows people of modest means to satisfy most of their basic demands. The living conditions of the average family illustrate the means by which material limitations have been minimized. Families are large and houses small; hence privacy within the household is nonexistent. Yet a fenced enclosure containing house and yard offers each family its aloofness and individuality. Except in city slums, each has its miniature garden. Long-standing customs eliminate the need for elaborate furnishings, for Japanese do not find it uncomfortable to sit or sleep on their floor mats of padded straw. Removal of shoes in houses keeps floors clean enough to make this possible. The Japanese bathe often—daily, if water and fuel permit—at home or, for those too poor to have the facilities in their houses, in inexpensive public baths. Lest the close-knit, authoritarian families appear unbearably austere, it should be stressed that they are built on affection, particularly for children, to as great an extent as in any society. The fond parent, overindulgent toward his small children, is as typical in fact as in folklore. Sternness toward one's children comes only at the age in their lives when they may be expected to shoulder the responsibilities of adulthood. As for the possibilities of genuine affection between husbands and wives who started their married life as complete strangers to one another, one can only point out that unhappy marriages seem no commoner than under any other system.

To the limit of their economic circumstances, the Japanese love to travel. Family cars are next to nonexistent and roads unsuited to automobile travel, but railroads go within a few miles of almost every point in Japan and offer the people one of their characteristic diversions. Sightseeing in historic or scenic places, mountain-climbing, and skiing are popular enough to make tourism more than just a major "export industry." It is a domestic industry as well.

A word on health and sanitation: overcrowding, diet deficiencies, and inadequate sanitary facilities make for a serious public health problem requiring all the resources of Japan's advanced medical science to keep under control. The incidence of tuberculosis is high, while heroic efforts have been required on a few occasions since the war to prevent typhus and smallpox outbreaks from reaching serious epidemic proportions. Diseases of sanitation are common, owing partly to the use of night soil as fertilizer. For reasons of economy, sudden substitution of a safer sewage disposal system would create more serious problems than it would solve. On the brighter side, stand-ards of medical techniques and equipment are high, and the relatively new science of public health continues to make prog-ress in improving the nation's health. Noticeable reduction since the war of the death rate from tuberculosis is only one of several comparable accomplishments.

LANGUAGE

Linguists assign Japanese to a language family by itself. Only one other language is obviously related to it, that of the Ryukyu Islands, which is so closely related that it may be considered a dialect of Japanese. Hence there is no really convincing evidence as to the origins of the language. Many attempts have been made to relate Japanese to the language families of Asia as well as to the Malayo-Polynesian group. Similarities of structure to these seem more than accidental, but students still hesitate to consider them conclusive evidence of linguistic kin-ship. Chinese is completely unlike Japanese in structure and native vocabulary, though modern Japanese has thousands of words borrowed from Chinese just as modern English has countless words of Latin or Greek derivation. The common misapprehension that Japanese is similar linguistically to Chi-nese is explained by the accident that Japanese is written with Chinese characters.

Chinese loan words in Japanese include many signifying things or concepts unknown to the primitive Japanese people. Some, such as *fude,* "writing brush," and *uma,* "horse," became fully naturalized Japanese words at a very early date, while others, such as *bōzu,* "Buddhist priest," and *seiji,* "government," represent borrowing at a more advanced state of Japanese civilization. An interesting class of Chinese derivatives in modern Japanese contains words coined in Japan to meet the demands of modern science and technology. Examples are *jidôsha,* "automobile," from three Chinese elements meaning self-moving vehicle, and *mannen-hitsu,* "fountain pen," meaning "ten-thousand-year brush."

The Japanese have adapted the Chinese characters to their own language in an ingenious, but unwieldy, way. Japanese words with close equivalents in Chinese—most nouns, verbs, and adjectives—are written with the appropriate Chinese characters. Particles and other grammatical devices having no exact equivalents in Chinese are represented phonetically with symbols called *kana,* which the Japanese themselves invented by modifying certain of the Chinese ideographs. Each of the forty-eight *kana* represents a syllable, and one could, if one wished, write Japanese exclusively by means of them. Marked benefits seem possible from such a system, for *kana* orthography exhibits none of the vagaries of English, or even French, spelling. The possible benefits of adopting a phonetic system, either *kana* or the Roman alphabet, seem so obvious, in fact, that non-Japanese frequently ask just why it has never been tried. At such a question there ensues a passionate argument on the language reform issue, the Japanese siding almost unanimously, but almost alone, against reform. The reformers point out the following advantages to be gained:

1. The long hours Japanese school children spend learning to read and write their own language could be better spent at content courses in the natural and social sciences or the humanities.

2. The mechanics of printing and typing would be greatly simplified.

3. A common system of writing with Western countries would facilitate Japanese study of Western languages and hence Western culture.

4. Japanese technical and scientific writings, now all but unknown to Western scholars, would be more readily available to them.

In answer, the Japanese point out that:

1. A switch to a new system would within a generation make the classics of their own literature unavailable to them.

2. It would block them off from the civilization of China.

3. It would necessitate troublesome modification of their own language, for the diversity of the Chinese characters allows a larger vocabulary in written Japanese than the overly simple sound system permits in speech.

4. It would be an unnecessary inconvenience for a country already 99 percent literate to change anything so habitual as a writing system.

INTELLECTUAL LIFE

Japan's publishing industry is one of the world's largest and most vigorous. The Japanese as a whole are great readers and, as a consequence, a wide range of reading material is available to the public at remarkably low prices. Public libraries are comparatively new in Japan and as yet satisfy only a tiny fraction of the demand for popular books.

There is no limit to the range of subjects about which Japanese read. It is to be expected that American and European affairs, manners, customs, and civilization have been consuming interests in all classes of Japanese society since the advent of westernization nearly a century ago. Books on all phases of their own national life are equally popular.

Middle and higher schools stress the study of literature, and their graduates are as a rule well read in the classics of East and West. The novels of nineteenth-century Russia and of twentieth-century France are especially popular, though there has been an increase in interest in English and American fiction since the war. Translations of literature from all the major European languages exist in great number; some popular works have been translated many times. Japan has only recently become a signatory to the International Copyright Agreement, so that most of the existing translations, even those from living authors, were produced at lower costs than in the case of native books.

Japanese literature makes use of all the native conventions and traditions, though it has been influenced to a considerable degree by European literature. The average quality is perhaps no higher than anywhere else. Magazines cater to a wide range of interest—scholarly, technical, popular, and political.

Two or three of the Tokyo and Osaka dailies have circulations among the highest of any newspapers in the world. The severe postwar shortage of newsprint has not entirely abated, with the result that even the largest metropolitan papers are limited to six to eight pages per issue. The range of coverage in the dailies of national circulation is substantially the same as in America, news of national and international significance all but crowding out stories of purely local interest to the cities in which they are published. In addition, there are many feature stories, columns on homemaking, entertainment, fine arts, and finance, and editorials. A large number of provincial papers specialize in local news. In 1954 the dailies in Japan had a combined circulation of 34,271,000.

Japanese scientists compete on terms of equality with those of the rest of the world and many have been noteworthy contributors to world scientific knowledge at the highest level. There have been outstanding contributors in all the branches of physical and biological science as well as mathematics. The list includes, among many others, the chemist Takamine Jôkichi, who first synthesized adrenalin in 1901; Noguchi Hideyo, a doctor who made important contributions to the pathology of yellow fever and syphilis; and the Nobel Prize-winning physicist, Yukawa Hideki, whose prediction of the meson paved the way for later experimental confirmation.

READINGS

Benedict, Ruth. *The Chrysanthemum and the Sword; Patterns of Japanese Culture*. Boston, Houghton Mifflin, 1946.
Ishimoto, Shidzue. *Facing Two Ways; the Story of My Life*. New York, Farrar and Rinehart, 1935.
Sugimoto, Etsu. *A Daughter of the Samurai*. Garden City, Doubleday, Page, 1925.
Vining, Elizabeth Gray. *Windows for the Crown Prince*. Philadelphia, Lippincott, 1952.

FILMS

The Japanese Family. International Film Foundation, Inc., 1 East 42nd Street, New York 17, N.Y.
Kimono. Japan Travel Information Office, 10 Rockefeller Plaza, New York 20, N.Y.
Tooru's People. Religious Film Association, 45 Astor Place, New York 3, N.Y.

FINE ARTS

The main line of the Japanese artistic tradition dates from shortly after the introduction of Buddhism from the Continent in the sixth century of the Christian era. All the major fine arts in Japan—painting, sculpture, and architecture—took their first inspirations from the traditions, already refined and sophisticated when they reached Japan, of India, China, and Korea. Art of succeeding periods continued to be influenced by new developments on the mainland, though Japan's increased isolation from the rest of the Far East from the ninth to the fourteenth centuries encouraged her artists to apply their own native genius to the borrowed tradition. The most vigorous Japanese art of the past three or four centuries is obviously related to the art of China, but much that is most characteristic about it is wholly Japanese.

Buddhism has played much the same role in the development of Japanese art that Christianity has in the European artistic tradition. For a long while most of the art patronage and much of the actual skill and knowledge in artistic techniques were provided by the Buddhist monasteries in Japan or by missionary priests from abroad. As a result, the subject matter of Japanese art in this period was predominantly religious—aspects of the Buddha or incidents of his life, Buddhist divinities and holy men, and scenes from the religious life of the people. Even when at a later date Japanese painters began to specialize in landscapes, portraiture, and other kinds of secular art, many of them were priests who depended on monastic institutions for their training and livelihood. Even the secular works of such artists frequently illustrate in subtle fashion Buddhist ways of thought.

Buddhist art and the classical art in imitation of Chinese styles both reflected the tastes of the Japanese upper classes. Parallel to this sort of aristocratic art, there existed a tradition of folk arts and crafts predominantly secular and designed for the appreciation of the middle classes. The woodblock prints of the seventeenth, eighteenth, and nineteenth centuries were works of this kind, produced in great quantity and reckoned of no lasting value; yet they were works of skilled craftsmanship and artistic sophistication. Similarly, minor arts such as textiles and ceramics displayed technical virtuosity and aesthetic taste, even when designed for the enjoyment of humble folk.

ANCIENT ART (TO CA. 600 A.D.)

Pre-Buddhist art in Japan is of more than purely archaeological interest, though the techniques were primitive and the range of subject matter narrow. Copper and bronze utensils indicate early (*ca.* first century) knowledge from the Asiatic continent of casting techniques.

Ancient artifacts have been found chiefly in or near the burial mounds of the period, indicating a ritual significance for these works. (If nonritual art objects existed, they have not been preserved.) Finds include tools and weapons of stone and metal, pottery, jewels, and rude clay figures of men and animals, known as *haniwa*.

More or less intelligent guesses as to the nature of the earliest architecture have been made from non-Chinese elements in traditional Japanese houses and shrines and from ancient temple buildings of distinctive style that have been repaired and rebuilt continually since unrecorded antiquity. Ancient buildings were probably of wood or bamboo construction with rain-resistant reed or bark roofs and raised floors.

ART OF THE EARLY BUDDHIST PERIOD (TO CA. 800)

Many splendid examples of Buddhist sculpture of this period have been preserved in temples and monasteries. Those of the sixth and seventh centuries are of wood or bronze, whereas eighth-century pieces include some of clay or dry lacquer. There is little suitable stone, either for sculpture or as building material, in Japan. Statues are stylized and symbolic rather than literally representational, though the best examples give no feeling of naïveté or of clumsy technique. Pieces range in scale from devotional images a few inches high to the 53-foot bronze Buddha in the Tôdai-ji in Nara.

Such architecture as remains from the period consists largely in temple buildings of Chinese style. The main hall (Kon-dô) and pagoda of the Hôryû-ji near Nara are the oldest wooden buildings in the world. They are of special interest to students of oriental architecture, since constant repairing has splendidly preserved them as specimens of the Chinese wooden temple construction no longer extant on the Continent.

Painting was an adjunct to religious architecture. The best extant pieces are the suavely stylized panel scenes on the Tamamushi-zushi, a small shrine in the Hôryû-ji, and the murals of divinities and bodhisattvas in the main hall of the same temple. (The last-named paintings, well preserved for twelve centuries, were extensively damaged by fire in 1949.)

The minor arts such as metalwork, textiles, musical instruments, and ceramics were appreciated in Japan of the Nara period. The collection now preserved in the Shôsô-in Imperial Treasury in Nara are unrivaled examples of the craftsmanship of the eighth-century civilizations of China and even Persia. Many of the pieces were undoubtedly imported to Japan, though many others were of Japanese manufacture.

HEIAN ART (800–1200)

The removal of the capital to Kyoto in 794 marked only a minor break in the artistic tradition. Buddhism remained the major Japanese religion of the upper classes, and the fine arts continued to be patronized by the clergy or by pious laymen. A more important influence on Japanese art was the gradual cessation of direct official relations with China. The political power of the culturally brilliant T'ang dynasty in China was in dissolution after the late eighth century. The dynasty fell in 906. The last of many embassies to China of Japanese priests, officials, and artists was in 838. Thereafter, for more than five hundred years, the only intercourse between the two countries was occasional unofficial visits by priests or traders. Japan was never in complete isolation from the artistic influence of the Continent, but Japanese artists did cultivate greater originality during this period than before. Sculpture of the Heian period is similar in forms and content to the earlier pieces, though it is much inferior in vigor.

Architecture also suffered for a time from the cessation of fresh stimulation from China. One of the few remaining masterworks from the period is the Phoenix Hall (Hôô-dô) of the Byôdô-in at Uji, a temple dating from 1056. The attenuated symmetry of the roof lines suggests to some the delicate balance of a poised bird and is a mark of a more native Japanese taste.

The Heian period produced the first paintings of a new and completely Japanese manner known as *Yamato-e*. These scrolls and painted fans and ornaments are secular in feeling, take their subject matter from the everyday life of people of all classes, and exhibit great animation and grace of composition. Many of the Buddhist paintings of the Heian period are masterpieces of world rank.

KAMAKURA ART (1200–1400)

Social and religious changes that accompanied the advent of feudal government at Kamakura in the late twelfth century altered the role of the arts in contemporary life. The new aristocracy were no longer effete courtiers but military men of simple, vigorous tastes. The flourishing Buddhist sects of the period were less philosophically abstruse and of greater appeal to the common people, and reflected in their artistic canons the same simplicity and directness that characterized their tenets of belief.

In the thirteenth century, Japanese sculpture achieved its last and greatest virtuosity. Unkei (twelfth to thirteenth century) and his school produced wooden religious images and portrait statues ranging in expression from the greatest violence to the most serene spirituality. Anatomical faithfulness to nature gives these works an appearance of "realism" in contrast to the frank stylizations of earlier sculpture.

The giant bronze Buddha (Daibutsu) at Kamakura dates from 1252. Even so technically unwieldy a form as this exemplifies the expressiveness that Kamakura sculptors mastered.

The earliest Japanese Zen monasteries date from the thirteenth century and are of a newly imported, unostentatious style in keeping with the tenets of the sect. Dwellings of the feudal aristocracy were fortresses and, like the Zen temples, were of tasteful simplicity.

Kamakura painting is distinguished for the variety of its themes and the vigor and realism with which they are portrayed. Religious scenes skillfully use fire, cloud, and landscape background not as mere ornament but to heighten the emotional qualities of the composition. Landscapes of familiar Japanese places were early instances of the imparting of spiritual qualities to wholly secular subject matter. Priests, legendary Buddhist patriarchs, and even supernatural beings emerge from the religious art of the period as individuals, and the portraits of contemporary personages (such as that of Minamoto Yoritomo, who founded the Kamakura shogunate) are masterpieces of personality suggestion. Most impressive of all the Kamakura paintings perhaps are the scrolls (*emaki-mono*) illustrating many kinds of religious and secular narrative. Their

styles are as varied as the subjects represented. Most of them are
further developments of the *Yamato-e* style.

MUROMACHI ART (1400–1568)

The political disunity that prevailed under the later Ashikaga
shoguns was no deterrent to the brilliance of the arts they patronized. Indeed, shoguns like Ashikaga Yoshimasa (reigned
1449–74) seem to have allowed their love of elegance and
luxury to divert attention from the really pressing problems
of the time, those of endemic warfare and political dissolution.
Rulers of the Ashikaga family built the period's two most
noteworthy architectural monuments, the Golden Pavilion
(Kinkaku-ji, destroyed by fire in 1950 but since reconstructed)
and the Silver Pavilion (Ginkaku-ji), as residences. The former
dated from 1397, was of unostentatious taste except for the
gilt of its interior apartments, and merged with complete success into its garden setting. The Silver Pavilion achieved elegance through an even greater restraint approaching plainness.

The artistic canons of the Zen sect were a healthful influence
on painting in the Muromachi period, for at the same time that
they encouraged the strictest economy in the use of line and
color, they freed the talents of Zen painters for the widest
variety of themes. Formal devotional images and scenes from
the supernatural never again found much favor among either
artists or patrons of art. They gave way to landscapes, nature
studies, and scenes from secular life. Japanese artists of the
Muromachi period carried on a great Chinese painting tradition that dated from the Sung dynasty (tenth to thirteenth

centuries). Josetsu and Shûbun were early fifteenth-century masters of the Japanese ink-painting style that culminated a hundred years later in the work of Sesshû (1420–1506) and his school. The Kano school, a more native adaptation of the Sung landscape tradition, stemmed from the work of two Muromachi painters, Kano Masanobu (1434–1530) and Kano Motonobu (1476–1559).

MOMOYAMA ART (1568–1615)

Momoyama is an area in the southern environs of Kyoto where Toyotomi Hideyoshi erected a fortress-palace in 1594. The architectural monuments of the period to which it gave its name were lavishly decorated and of impressive scale, reflecting not only the wealth of their builders, of whom the low-born Hideyoshi was typical, but also their standards of taste, untutored and unrefined in comparison with those of the Muromachi aristocrats. The sixteenth-century introduction to Japan of Western firearms necessitated a type of fortress similar in construction to contemporary European castles. Japanese architects combined the European principles of defense with characteristically oriental features of design to produce the many castles of the period. The castle at Himeji (1581) is a well-preserved example of this unique form. The gigantic keep of the Osaka castle was rebuilt in 1931, but it is faithful in external details to Hideyoshi's original fortress on the same site. Specimens of walls, moats, and out-buildings from castles no longer intact may be seen in the Imperial Palace in Tokyo and at the site of the Nagoya castle.

Gardens too were of unprecedented magnificence. The Japanese art of landscape gardening was never used to create formally patterned gardens of the European fashion but instead aimed as far as possible at the reproduction of natural landscape beauty, often at prodigious expense of labor and materials.

Momoyama painting was opulent and ostentatious. Wholly secularized under the patronage of the great military rulers, it abandoned the economy and subtlety of the Muromachi schools, preserving their exquisite craftsmanship and sense of design. Dazzlingly colorful screen-paintings of flowers, birds, and landscapes were commissioned by the score as ornaments for Momoyama palaces.

Japanese ceramic art had been encouraged by the vogue for the tea ceremony that started in the fifteenth century. The semiritual nature of the ceremony as originally practiced by devotees of Zen called for extreme austerity of design in the bowls and utensils used. An art was made of achieving the proper degree of roughness and gracelessness, with the paradoxical result that some of the least prepossessing of the Muromachi art objects (to the untrained eye) soon came to be esteemed as priceless masterworks. The spirit of the Momoyama period, however, disdained economy and called for show. The ornate and colorful bowls and dishes typical of that time opened the way for a great variety of graceful and useful ceramic objects in the following period.

TOKUGAWA ART (1615–1868)

The age of the Tokugawa shoguns was one of peace, of gradual decrease in the vitality of the Buddhist sects, and of the growth of cities and a prosperous merchant class. While the art of the classic schools tended to decline still further in originality and strength, popular arts and folkcrafts flourished as never before with the patronage of city-dwelling samurai and merchants.

While Buddhist architecture fell into repetitions of old styles and increasingly elaborate products of Momoyama decorativeness (for example, the gorgeously carved and painted but overly fussy temples at Nikkô), one branch of architecture reached new heights of formal clarity and functional efficiency. This was domestic architecture, a hybrid development from native and Chinese elements.

Schools of painting proliferated in the seventeenth century. The Kano school broke up into several traditions, each with its unique qualities; the decorative art of the Momoyama period influenced several major Tokugawa artists, of whom Kôrin (1658–1716) is best known; the *Yamato-e* tradition produced an important new school, the Sumiyoshi, that was to be a forerunner of the woodblock print schools of the eighteenth and nineteenth centuries. Western painting was known to the Japanese as early as the mid-sixteenth century and in the seventeenth inspired a minor school in partial imitation of it, specializing in scenes of Japanese commerce with westerners. Maruyama Ôkyo (1733–95) introduced a new realism in his studies of birds and animals and established a school influenced to some extent by Western illustration.

Most celebrated of the Tokugawa arts is that of *ukiyo-e,* the paintings and block prints designed for mass distribution to city dwellers of all social classes. In the latter part of the seventeenth century print artists such as Hishikawa Moronobu (d. *ca.* 1694) and Torii Kiyonobu (1664–1729) began to manufacture pictures of actors, a type of *ukiyo-e* that was to become one of the most characteristic. The early prints were in black and white but were sometimes hand-colored. Color printing was invented about 1741 and full-color printing about 1765. More sophisticated use of the block-cutting techniques and greater freedom of design and subject matter in the latter part of the eighteenth century led the art to its culmination under such masters as Harunobu (1724–70), Utamaro (1754–1806), and Sharaku (painted 1794–95). Sharaku specialized entirely in theatrical prints and was a master caricaturist. Hokusai (1760–1849) and Hiroshige (1797–1858) were artists of originality and integrity in an age when the art as a whole had begun to decline.

Brief mention should be made of the countless objects of everyday use that became works of art at the hands of Tokugawa craftsmen: pottery, brass or iron utensils, folk-toys, fans, lacquer trays, boxes and tobacco pouches, *netsuke* (carved wood or ivory pendants), and the like.

MODERN ART (SINCE 1868)

The masters of the *ukiyo-e* created Japan's last great art of a distinctive and indigenous style. There have been many innovations in the hundred years or so since the death of Hokusai and Hiroshige, and they have literally revolutionized the fine arts, but all these innovations have been of Western, not Eastern, origin. The process of westernization began late in the Tokugawa period in the prints and paintings of artistic radicals like Shiba Kôkan (1747–1818) and Watanabe Kazan (1793–1841), both of whom experimented with scientific laws of perspective and other approaches to realism. The craze for westernization during the Meiji period (1868–1912) brought to the attention of the Japanese all the achievements of Western art, allowing them to go the limit in slavish imitation of a myriad of its varieties. The result was often an affront to the taste of both civilizations, but in the long run such a mingling of traditions produced much fine work by Japanese artists. A contrary process by which Western artists in the latter part of the nineteenth century discovered the values of Japanese painting and decorative arts brought the traditions of the two cultures still closer together, eventuating in a contemporary art in Japan that is not so much Western as international.

READINGS

Fenollosa, Ernest Francisco. *Epochs of Chinese and Japanese Art; an Outline History of Asiatic Design.* New and rev. ed. with copious notes by Professor Petrucci, 2 vols. New York, Stokes, 1921.

Henderson, H. G., and R. T. Paine, Jr. *The University Prints. Series O, Section III. Japanese Art.* Newton, Mass., The University Prints, 1939.

Minamoto, H. *An Illustrated History of Japanese Art.* Translated by Harold G. Henderson. Kyoto, Hoshino, 1935.

Tsuda, Noritake. *Handbook of Japanese Art.* Tokyo, Sanseidô, 1935.

Warner, Langdon. *The Enduring Art of Japan.* Cambridge, Harvard University Press, 1952.

FILMS

Advancing Kyoto. Japan Travel Information Office, 10 Rockefeller Plaza, New York 20, N.Y.

Ancient Sculpture of Japan. Japan Travel Information Office, 10 Rockefeller Plaza, New York 20, N.Y.

Ceramics of Japan. Information Section of the Embassy of Japan, 2514 Massachusetts Ave., N.W., Washington 8, D.C.

Conspiracy in Kyoto. Indiana University, Division of Adult Education and Public Services, Audio-Visual Center, Bloomington, Indiana.

LITERATURE

The poetry and prose of Japan have throughout history been under a certain debt to the literature of China. Several features, however, have been wholly Japanese. For example, the novel had an independent development in Japan, actually maturing earlier there than it did in China; indigenous elements in the Japanese drama created two unique forms of theater, the *nô* and the *kabuki;* in addition, differences between the Chinese and Japanese languages made for wide variance between the poetic forms of the two countries. Modern Japan has borrowed heavily from the forms, themes, and techniques of Western literature, though certain native traits have retained their popularity with contemporary writers. In particular, Japanese poetry of traditional style and a characteristic type of informal essay, called *zuihitsu,* continue to occupy important places in the literary scene.

Terseness is a frequently cited characteristic of Japanese literature; long poems are rare, and long prose works are, with some notable exceptions, collections of more or less independent fragments or episodes. Many Western commentators have noted that the emotional range of Japanese poetry and prose fiction is comparatively limited; repressed love, sorrows of parting, world-weariness, and the apprehension of earthly evanescence loom large among their themes. Japanese writers often framed these sentiments in language of the greatest subtlety and delicacy but rarely transcended them into the realms more esteemed in Western writing of personalized passion or tragedy. Yet the finest Japanese literature succeeds in being spirited and moving to the very degree that the casualness and indirection of its expression suggest the writer's convictions about the universal human issues of aspiration, contention, resignation, love, and death.

EARLY POETRY

The primitive Japanese language had no alphabet; the earliest literature consisted in rituals and chronicles preserved for an indeterminate number of years in an oral tradition before finally being written down about the seventh or eighth century.

A few secular verses from ancient times have been incorporated into the earliest chronicles. A far more important collection of early poetry, however, is the *Man'yô-shû* (Collection of a Myriad Leaves) compiled toward the close of the Nara period. There are more than four thousand poems in the collection, most of them dating from the seventh and eighth centuries. The *Man'yô-shû* was compiled under the auspices of the Imperial Court and reflects the outlook of the aristocracy of the time. A few songs of the nature of folk poetry deal with peasant life; other poems make reference to the life of border guards stationed in the distant eastern provinces. These help round out the picture the collection gives of the social life of the age. The poems are mostly short, occasional lyrics of fresh, sensuous language. Rhyme has no place in Japanese poetry. Instead, the *Man'yô-shû*—in common with most later poetry— makes use of patterns of line length to provide formal regularity. The most common pattern alternates five-syllable and seven-syllable lines, finishing with an additional line of seven syllables, thus: 5, 7, 5, 7 . . . 5, 7, 7. The classic form is the *tanka,* or brief poem, of five lines in the pattern 5, 7, 5, 7, 7.

There were many later collections of verse of the general style of the *Man'yô-shû,* the most famous being the *Kokin-shû* (Collection of Poems, Ancient and Modern), of the early tenth century, and *Shin-kokin-shû,* of the early thirteenth.

CLASSIC PROSE

Native Japanese prose was in some respects an outgrowth of poetry. The earliest prose masterwork in Japanese is the preface to the *Kokin-shû,* written by its compiler, Ki-no-Tsurayuki (882–946), and dealing with the nature of poetry. Early works of fiction consisted of narratives interspersed with verses that expressed in terse form the emotional flavor of the story. There is some reason to believe that such collections were thought of primarily as anthologies of poems and that the narratives that fill them out were meant to be explanations of the verse parts. Leaving aside the primitive legends and other narratives that are to be found in the early chronicles, the principal milestones of the development of Japanese fiction are the *Taketori Monogatari* (The Bamboo-Cutter's Tale), an extended fairy tale of the ninth century, and the *Ise Monogatari* (Tales of Ise) and *Yamato Monogatari* (Tales of Yamato), of the tenth century.

Supplementing supernatural and poetical fiction were other prose works of an informal nature: travel diaries and notebooks of brief anecdotes and impressions. Such forms were considered appropriate to the Japanese language, whereas more ponderous works of the same age were customarily written in Chinese, the prestige language. The impressive number of women who contributed to the development of Japanese prose stems from the curious feature in the social structure that made Chinese the language of government, religion, and classical learning—in short, the literary language for men. Ki-no-Tsurayuki freely admitted that in writing the *Kokin-shû* preface and the *Tosa Nikki* (best known of the Heian travel diaries), he was adopting the "women's language," that is to say, Japanese. The best of the literary notebooks is the *Makura no Sôshi* (Pillow Book) of Sei Shônagon, a court lady who wrote about 1000 A.D. It is filled with perceptive, elegantly phrased comments on art, human nature, and the workings of court society.

The *Genji Monogatari* (Tale of Genji) by Murasaki Shikibu, another court lady and a contemporary of Sei Shônagon, is a narrative of the refined court life with which Lady Murasaki was familiar. Like earlier fictional works it abounds in verses dashed off by its characters in moments of emotional stress in lieu of the inelegant bluntness of prose speech. Unlike all previous Japanese works, it unfolds a single sustained story in which the characters behave from motivations of lifelike complexity. It is, in fact, the first true Japanese novel and has been called, moreover, the world's first great work of prose fiction. It is ostensibly a biography of a brilliant sensualist, Prince Genji, whose lifetime of amatory adventures amid sur-

roundings of luxury and refinement aptly illustrates the
themes dominant in Japanese literature of the illusoriness of
pleasure and the transience of the material world.

THE WRITING OF HISTORY

The Japanese learned their historiography from China and
contributed little that was new to it. Early in the Nara period
(eighth century) the Court ordered the ancient legends and
chronicles of Japan to be compiled and set down in Japanese.
These were the *Kojiki*, or "Chronicles of Ancient Events." Six
official histories in the Chinese language documented the history of the Imperial Court down to about 900. These were the
so-called six national histories, all of them of an unadorned
chronological style. History became an important branch of
literature later in the Heian period with a number of works of
colorful narrative style. Some of these, like the *Ô-Kagami* (a
biography of the eleventh-century regent Fujiwara Michinaga),
were chronicles of court life; others, like the *Heike Monogatari*
(Tales of the Heike), which dealt with the interclan wars of
the twelfth century, were primarily battle accounts. His-
torians of the feudal Middle Ages (thirteenth to sixteenth
centuries) combined the narrative interest of these chronicles
with political or moral purpose. Kitabatake Chikafusa (1293–
1354) typified this sort of history in the *Jinnô-shôtô-ki* (Chroni-
cle of the True Dynasty), written during the dynastic schism of
the fourteenth century; Chikafusa aimed to prove the justice
of the southern dynasty's claims to legitimacy. The Tokugawa
era produced a number of histories based on formal Chinese
models. One of them, the *Honchô Tsugan*, compiled by the

official academy of the shogun's court, was a strictly chronological general history of Japan. Another, the *Dai-Nihon-shi,*
or "History of Japan," was arranged topically in the manner
of the official dynastic histories of China. It was written by
scholars at the court of the fief of Mito and supported the notion, familiar to students of recent Japanese history, of the
sacred character of the Imperial dynasty.

THE NÔ DRAMA

Japanese classic drama grew out of Shinto or Buddhist ritual
dance-plays of Nara and Heian times. In the fourteenth century a group of entertainers with the patronage of the Ashikaga
shoguns brought together elements from the old theater and
refined them into a highly stylized dramatic form known as
nô. It is drama of the greatest austerity, understatement being
its dominating feature in text, staging, and performance. The
brief poetic plays usually underline a Buddhist or, more rarely,
Shinto moral and often feature supernatural events and characters. Often the events that constitute the drama are not acted
on the stage at all but are described by their protagonists as
having taken place years earlier. Actors eke out the extremely
limited range of bodily gesture permitted by the classic canons
with dances suggestive of the feeling of the drama while
choruses reminiscent of those in Greek drama relate or am-
plify the action from the side of the stage. The performance of
these plays is of too recondite a character to have retained a
great modern following even among Japanese, though the
texts are still greatly appreciated in Japan for their moral
loftiness and poetic beauty.

TOKUGAWA THEATER

The urban and middle-class culture of the seventeenth and eighteenth centuries brought forth new dramatic forms of far greater popular appeal than the aristocratic nô dramas. The most important of these from the literary point of view was the *jôruri* theater, in which the action was carried out as realistically as possible on a stage by puppets about half life-size and the dialogue and choric commentary intoned from the side by a single performer known as the *jôruri*. The plays themselves were often adaptations of nô dramas, but the language was modernized and colloquial, and the performance, save that it was by dolls rather than people, was more realistic in every respect. The best-known dramatist was Chikamatsu Monzaemon (1653–1725).

The kabuki drama was a further step in the direction of theatrical realism. Performed by live actors on huge stages, usually with elaborate scenery and brilliant costumes, it nevertheless retains some of the stylizations of its predecessors, nô and the doll-dramas. Some of the artificialities of performance, in fact, are conscious imitations of the halting, awkward movements of puppets. The plays are often mere adaptations of those used in the puppet theater, but elaboration by generations of actors has made the best known of them much longer than the seventeenth-century originals. Single plays sometimes last the better part of a day. The artistic distinction of the kabuki theater lies not in the literary qualities of the plays but in the brilliance of the acting tradition. As hybrid productions of dialogue, music, and the dance, they can be quite effective theater, and it is this fact that has preserved the kabuki as the only truly living branch of Japan's classic theatrical art.

HAIKU AND SENRYÛ

The *tanka* verse form lost popularity in the seventeenth century to another still briefer and more indirect type of expression. This was the *haiku,* a three-line form of seventeen syllables in the arrangement 5, 7, 5. By convention *haiku* were associated with seasons of the year, and their writers sought in them to evoke striking impressions of the qualities of nature with the greatest economy of words. So brief a form could hardly bring forth more than mere suggestions of poetic ideas, somewhat as though single lines from European lyric poetry were made to stand alone as complete poems. Even today practically all literate Japanese try their hand at the form at some time or other, though the greatest *haiku* poets were of the school of Bashô (1644–94).

Senryû were of the same length and syllabic arrangements as *haiku* but were humorous, satiric, or epigrammatic.

THE TOKUGAWA NOVEL

A revival of fiction during the Tokugawa period stemmed, as had the contemporary developments in the theater, from the diffusion of literate culture to members of the new townsman class. As in the case of the classic productions of the Heian period, short stories and novels played delicately or indelicately with themes of unrequited and illicit love. As Heian fiction dealt largely with the aristocratic class for whose consumption it was written, so that of the Tokugawa period concerned the lives of the merchant class that read it. Ibara Saikaku (1642–93) wrote the most highly esteemed novels of the period, colloquial, poetic, and flavorful.

MODERN DEVELOPMENTS

The enormous range of Western literature first came to the attention of the Japanese late in the nineteenth century and inspired countless imitations of almost every one of its varieties. Adaptation of European naturalistic drama to Japanese themes involved a violent wrenching away from the conventions to which the Japanese were accustomed in their own theater. Similarly, the evolution of types of fiction that would simultaneously satisfy the public's old taste for the evocative and its new demand for complex and sustained narratives dealing with psychological and social themes has not been easy. The Meiji period was one of experimentation; one immediate problem was the substitution of natural, colloquial language for the archaic literary style that prevailed in formal writing. The recurring themes of Meiji novels are Japan's destiny in the world, the acceptance of new standards of social justice, and the fierce struggle in the minds of Japanese intellectuals between the old ways of the East and the new ones of the West. Futabatei Shimei was an early realist among Meiji novelists, creating almost plotless psychological descriptions of life in the upper middle class, which was most touched by westernization. Higuchi Ichiyô, the foremost woman writer of modern Japan, wrote realistic novels subtly suggesting the difficulties of psychological adjustment to the greater fluidity of Meiji society.

In the years immediately following the turn of the century, a number of younger Japanese novelists struck out in reaction to the mid-Meiji predisposition to crudely realistic treatments of social and political issues. Shimazaki Tôson wrote naturalistic problem novels of society, but the problems were presented in intimate psychological terms, and psychology became and remained the center of interest in Japanese fiction. Natsume Sôseki, writing between 1905 and 1914, used a variety of styles: realistic, as in *Kokoro,* a tragic story of an intellectual forced by his own devotion to everyday obligations into a pointless and thwarted life; satiric, as in *Wagahai wa Neko de Aru* (I Am a Cat), whose feline narrator pokes fun at human ways; and casually poetic, as in *Kusa-makura,* a fictional travel diary in the manner of the informal prose works of the Heian period. Mori Ôgai, an army surgeon for whom fiction was an avocation, examined psychological—particularly sexual—behavior from the background of his scientific training and attempted to counteract the current tendency in fiction of overemphasizing the importance of romantic love.

The bitterly satiric short-story writer, Akutagawa Ryûnosuke, killed himself in 1927 when he was still a young man. He left a number of sardonic masterpieces similar in some respects to the allegories of his Czech contemporary, Franz Kafka. *Kappa* is a mock-utopian description of a society of super-rationalistic river-dwarfs carrying to their logical absurdity the materialistic tendencies that Akutagawa feared in his own society. *Yabu no Naka* (In a Grove), on which the motion picture *Rashômon* was based, by juxtaposing several accounts of the same murder, examined human claims to noble, unselfish action and found them to be hypocritical.

An idealistic school of which Mushakôji Saneatsu is a typical member has continued to apply the methods of past psychological fiction to situations illustrative of man's moral nature, feeling that the foremost duty of fiction is to point out the fundamental human obligation of sympathy.

An important development of recent decades has been the revival of some of the styles of classic Japanese prose, emphasizing their refinement of language and qualities of evanescent, sensuous beauty. Tanizaki Jun'ichirô has translated the *Genji Monogatari* into modern Japanese and tries in his own fiction to emulate Lady Murasaki's evocation of a serene and self-sufficient world. The westernized protagonist of one of Tanizaki's novels cultivates classic Japanese music in a forlorn attempt to escape the feverishness of twentieth-century urban life. In reaction to a spate of novels of social and moral significance, Tanizaki takes an amoral attitude toward life, finding aesthetic satisfaction in behavior that other writers could only find morally repugnant.

Postwar fiction cannot be easily summarized. Its most striking product is Tanizaki's *Sasame-Yuki* (Snowflakes), a vast and rambling tale of upper middle-class family life in prewar Osaka. Its great popularity is probably an index of the current need for escape from grim postwar realities, though other novelists continue to treat problems of current importance.

READINGS

Akutagawa, Ryûnosuke. *Rashômon, and Other Stories.* Translated by Takashi Kojima. New York, Liveright, 1952.

Bowers, Faubion. *Japanese Theatre*. Foreword by Joshua Logan. New York, Hermitage, 1952.

Dazai, Osamu. *The Setting Sun*. Translated by Donald Keene. Norfolk, Conn., New Directions, 1956.

Ernst, Earle. *The Kabuki Theatre*. New York, Oxford University Press, 1956.

Ihara, Saikaku. *Five Women Who Loved Love*. Translated by William Theodore de Bary. Rutland, Vermont, and Tokyo, Charles E. Tuttle Company, 1956.

Keene, Donald. *Japanese Literature; an Introduction for Western Readers*. London, John Murray, 1953.

Keene, Donald (comp. and ed.). *Anthology of Japanese Literature from the Earliest Era to the Mid-nineteenth Century*. New York, Grove Press, 1955.

—— *Modern Japanese Literature*. New York, Grove Press, 1956.

Kobayashi, Nobuko (trans.). *The Sketch-book of the Lady Sei Shônagon*. New York, Dutton, 1930.

Mishima, Yukio. *The Sound of Waves*. Translated by Meredith Weatherby. New York, Alfred A. Knopf, 1956.

Natsume, Sôseki. *Kokoro*. Translated by Ineko Satô. Tokyo, Hokuseidô, 1941.

Nippon Gakujutsu Shinkôkai. *The Manyôshû*. One Thousand Poems Selected and Translated from the Japanese. Tokyo, Iwanami, 1940.

Tanizaki, Jun'ichirô. *Some Prefer Nettles*. Translated by Edward G. Seidensticker. New York, Alfred A. Knopf, 1955.

Waley, Arthur. *Japanese Poetry, the "Uta."* Oxford, Clarendon Press, 1919; lithoprint ed., London, Lund Humphries, 1945.

Waley, Arthur (trans.). *The Tale of Genji*. New York, Literary Guild, 1935.

RELIGION AND PHILOSOPHY

Until recent times philosophy in Japan has been associated with one or other of the country's great religions. One cause, or perhaps effect, of this feature was that the energies of most Japanese with speculative turns of mind have always been devoted to the solution of practical problems of individual or social morality. As in the West, it has been felt that these interests were best served within the framework of an organized cult. Of Japan's three major faiths, one is native and the other two borrowed. The roots of modern Shinto may be found in the ritual practices of the primitive Japanese people. Buddhism originated in India but arrived in Japan from China and Korea in the sixth century of the Christian era. Confucianism was known to the Japanese from the earliest days of their intercourse with China but attained its greatest prestige in Japan only after about 1600. A fourth great religion, Christianity, came to Japan in the sixteenth century, was suppressed by the authorities from the seventeenth to the nineteenth, and acquired additional importance from the latter time on as one of the bearers of Western civilization.

BUDDHISM

Of all religions Buddhism occupies by far the most important place in the religious life of Japan. Its influence on the fine arts and on social institutions, which cannot be overemphasized, is described elsewhere in the present handbook. Japanese Buddhism shares its most important doctrinal features with the Buddhist faith in other parts of Asia. Those which serve to differentiate the religion from, for example, Christianity may be suggested from the following points of doctrine:

1. Buddhism is not theistic: it conceives of no supreme intelligence which created the universe and directs the affairs of man. Whatever absolute entity Buddhism recognizes comprises the universe as a whole, which is self-creating.

2. Buddhist ethics demand as the first human obligation sympathy for all beings. This sympathy should not be reserved solely for other men nor even for all other sentient beings but belongs properly to the entire universe, inanimate as well as animate.

3. The phenomena of the material universe are, to Buddhists, unreal, since they exist only relative to each other and limited by time. Attachment to things, therefore, is evil and the source of all suffering. Buddhist practices aim at freeing men from their earthly desires and preparing them by intellectual, psychological, or mystic means for "loss of self," that is, absorption into the undifferentiated real universe, independent of time and space. This loss of self is known as nirvana, or "extinction," and is the Buddhist salvation.

Though Buddhist philosophy is highly metaphysical and

recondite, the popularity of the faith in Japan depended on the appeal of some of its other features. Some sects (for example, the Shingon and Tendai sects, which flourished from the Heian era) emphasized ritualistic or magical means to salvation. A group of sects (Jôdo, Shin, and Ji) took as one of their principal objects of worship the supernatural being Amida, who deferred his own salvation in order to aid that of the rest of the suffering world. The Amidist sects thus appealed for popular support to the notion that salvation could be attained by dependence on the aid freely given by Amida. The Zen sect deprecated the efficacy of intellectual and contemplative means to salvation, insisting instead that enlightenment must come suddenly and might even be facilitated by an active life.

Japan's only native sect was that founded in the thirteenth century by Nichiren, who identified the salvation of the individual with the establishment of a Buddhist state and society. Unlike other Japanese sects, that of Nichiren is both nationalistic and intolerant of all other religions.

Since the Middle Ages Japanese Buddhism has undergone little doctrinal growth, and there has been considerable decline in the power and vitality of the faith as a whole. Still, over half of the population are at least nominally Buddhist.

CONFUCIANISM

The Confucian cult in China incorporated many of the features of the primitive tribal religion of the Chinese people. To these ritualistic elements centuries of thinkers added complex metaphysical and ethical doctrines, the end product being closer to the Western idea of a philosophic school than to that of a religion. Confucian social and political doctrines formed the theoretical basis for the Chinese state from about the time of Christ; they provided the justification for absolute Imperial rule and administration by a scholar class chosen on the basis of talent. They even allowed the right of revolution in case the sovereign should fail in his duties to the society. In theory some of these political notions underlay the conduct of Japanese government from the Heian period on, though they probably had little influence on its actual practice. Confucian ideas as to individual relationships in the family or in society had greater vitality in Japan. One idea that the Japanese made peculiarly their own was the emphasis on personal loyalty of servant to master or of subject to sovereign as transcending all other obligations. It was this mutual and unequal relationship tending to bolster the foundation of the state that appealed especially to Japanese rulers in Tokugawa times and made of Confucianism virtually the official cult. Administrators of government, both in the Bakufu and in the fiefs, were usually scholars trained in classical Chinese learning. Education of the aristocracy was the province of Confucian academies supported privately by leading philosophers or at the expense of the feudal governments. Several schools flourished at the time, the principal of which were as follows:

1. The Bakufu's own official school, descending from the rationalistic Chinese school of Chu Hsi, which dated from the twelfth century.

2. A school emphasizing personal, rather than political, ethics dating from the Ming scholar Wang Yang-ming (1472–1528).

3. The Ancient Texts School of Ogyû Sorai (1666–1728), which stressed the need for sound scholarship in the fundamental Confucian writings in order to detect and throw out the accretions of later commentators.

4. Schools of economic thinkers, generally employed by feudal rulers to help solve pressing current problems. Confucians of this type such as Arai Hakuseki (1657–1725) and Dazai Shundai (1680–1747) contributed much to Japanese knowledge of the workings of finance, exchange, and distribution.

5. A school of Confucian nationalists founded by Yamaga Sokô (1622–85), who attempted to merge Confucianism with aspects of the native cult, founding the code of military virtue known as *Bushidô*.

6. Another nationalistic school sponsored by the princes of Mito, who belonged to a collateral branch of the Tokugawa family. Unlike Yamaga Sokô, these scholars remained in the fold of orthodox Confucianism but applied the theories of the Chinese state cult to the Japanese Imperial dynasty.

Confucianism as a genuine religious sect is no longer of any importance in Japan, though the contributions of three hundred years of thinkers in the Confucian philosophic tradition remain an important strand in the thought of our own time.

SHINTO

Primitive Japanese religion was animistic, conceiving of supernatural beings controlling all the forces of nature and dwelling in all natural things. Propitiating evil spirits and expressing gratitude to good ones were the principal functions of worship, and the cult had no sacred texts and no formulated articles of faith. It was not until Buddhism came on the scene that people began to call the native cult Shinto, "The Way of the Gods," for up to that time there had been no need to distinguish it from any other faith.

Contacts between Buddhism and Shinto modified both religions. As the Buddhist faith is not as a rule intolerant of other cults, it was possible to explain Shinto divinities as merely spirits of the Buddhist pantheon and Shinto ritualistic practices as permissible means to enlightment. In this way the idea became accepted by some thinkers that the two faiths were simply different ways of expressing the same truth. Occasionally single temples would be built as houses of worship for both religions, just as elaborate dogmas were sometimes worked out to reconcile the apparent inconsistencies between them. This curious symbiosis between the two cults was known as *ryôbu-Shintô,* or dual Shinto. It is illustrative of the point of view Japanese take toward religion that they see no inconsistency in the same individual's embracing the tenets of two quite different faiths.

In time new Shinto sects sprang up that were not openly associated with any foreign religion. Most, however, bore marks of Japan's association with Buddhism, Confucianism, and, in the past hundred years, Christianity. Increased nationalistic feeling during the Tokugawa period stimulated close study of native institutions and the indigenous parts of the national character. Though some of this thought fitted into the scheme of one or another of the Confucian schools, an important group of thinkers of the eighteenth and early nineteenth centuries led a movement back to the un-sinicized native faith. Chief among them were Kamo Mabuchi (1697–1769), Motoori Norinaga (1730–1801), and Hirata Atsutane (1776–1843). The Meiji government recognized pure Shinto as the official state religion, even demanding certain ritual observances of devout adherents to other religions. In an attempt to dissociate Shinto from Buddhism, the government forced temples of the *ryôbu-Shintô* persuasion to declare unequivocally whether they were thenceforth to be considered Buddhist or Shinto. State Shinto was in many respects a political, rather than a religious, development, since it was officially cultivated by the government as a spur to patriotic and nationalistic feeling. Emperor worship was one of its features, as was the propagation of doctrines of expansionism and national self-determination. The Emperor himself symbolized the disestablishment of Shinto in 1946 by publicly denying his own divinity. Yet most Japanese could truthfully say at that time that they had never considered the Emperor a god in any Western sense. He was thought to be divine in terms of the primitive polytheistic cult of the Japanese people—a cult that saw divinity in all the manifestations of nature and society.

The Shinto sects were not abolished under the Allied occupation. Disestablishment simply meant that certain old state-supported shrines lost their government subsidization and were placed in the same legal position as the institutions of any other religion. Even Japanese Buddhists and some Christians still include observation of Shinto practices as part of their religious life.

Until late in the nineteenth century Christianity to the Japanese meant, by and large, Roman Catholicism. Intimations of sectarianism within Christianity came to Japan as early as the sixteenth century, but the Protestants with whom the Japanese came into contact—mostly English and Dutch merchants—were not proselytizers and left little influence on the religious life of Japan. Small societies of Catholics in Kyushu survived centuries of persecution during the Tokugawa period and still remain there.

Catholic, Protestant, and Orthodox missionaries went to Japan in increasing numbers after 1859. Full religious freedom was given to Christians in 1889. Japanese Christians numbered about 300,000 in 1940 and had increased to 477,000 by 1955. About 273,000 are Protestant. An attempt was made by Japanese Protestants during and after the war to reduce the sectarianism within their ranks. The Church of Christ in Japan is an amalgamated body representing several of the major Protestant sects in other countries, Lutherans and Episcopalians remaining the principal independent bodies.

READINGS

Anesaki, Masaharu. *History of Japanese Religion with Special Reference to the Social and Moral Life of the Nation*. London, Kegan Paul, 1930.

Bunce, William K. (ed.). *Religions in Japan: Buddhism, Shinto, Christianity*. Rutland, Vt., Tuttle, 1955.

Holtom, Daniel Clarence. *National Faith of Japan; a Study in Modern Shintô*. London, Kegan Paul, 1938.

Tsunoda, Ryusaku, and William Theodore de Bary (eds.). *Readings in Japanese Thought*. New York, Columbia University Press, to be published.